BOOKS BY JOHN W. (Jack) LAMBERT:

Military History

The Long Campaign, Sunflower U. Press, 1982; reprinted by Schiffer, 2006

The Pineapple Air Force, Phalanx, 1990; reprinted by Schiffer, 2006

Wildcats Over Casablanca, Phalanx, 1992

Sortie: A Bibliography of American Aviation Unit Histories, Phalanx, 1993

Low Level Attack: Pacific, Specialty Press, 1997

Bombs, Torpedoes and Kamikazes, Specialty Press, 1997

Low Level Attack: Mediterranean & Europe, Specialty Press, 1998

Atlantic Air War: Sub-Hunters vs. U-Boats, Specialty Press, 1999

Assault on the Empire, Specialty Press, 2000

Defenseless: Command Failure at Pearl Harbor, (with Norman Polmar), Motor Books International, 2003

The Great Pacific Air Offensive, Vol. 1, Return to the Philippines, Schiffer, 2005

The Great Pacific Air Offensive, Vol. 2, Severing the Empire's Lifeline, Schiffer, 2005

The Great Pacific Air Offensive, Vol. 3, On Japan's Doorstep, Schiffer, 2005

Eighth Air Force: Victory & Sacrifice, Schiffer, 2006

The 14th Fighter Group in World War II, Schiffer, 2008

Fiction

The Battle of Otter Tail County, North Star Press of St. Cloud, 2010

TROUBLED WATERS

Thirty Years in the River Business

By
Jack Lambert

ISBN: 9 780965395007
Copyright 2012, John Lambert
dclambert@comcast.net

Editing, layout and design by Riverwise Inc., riverwise.com

DEDICATION

To my beloved wife, Dolly, who suffered through this ordeal with me and still managed to raise three exceptional children.

.

Contents

CHAPTER 1

ON-THE-JOB TRAINING

It was August 1952 when I volunteered for the Mississippi River transportation business. You couldn't fill a thimble with what I knew about barges and towboats, but with the arrogant enthusiasm of a 23-year-old, I wasn't worried. I had just returned from four years of military service where, assisted by General MacArthur, I had prevented the communist hordes from engulfing the Republic of Korea. How tough could steamboating be? I would learn the hard way. It was what we called OJT in the U.S. Air Force — on the job training — without benefit of map or manual.

The site of Twin City Barge Co. (TCB) had just dried out after a flood, although the sewer-like odor still clung to the walls and floor of the small office near St. Paul's downtown airport. The spring flood of 1952 was a humdinger that barely exceeded the 1951 level and topped that whacking good flood of 1881. There may well have been bigger ones than the 81, but that was as far back as records were kept. In earlier centuries the natives would just have stepped from their caves and said, "Holy shit, what a lot of water!" But during the 1800s some genius had the technological acumen to draw a line on the sandstone cliffs to mark the height of the flood. But I digress. In my 30 years in the water transportation business I would learn more about floods than any man should be compelled to know.

The U.S. Army Corps of Engineers, responsible for the operation of the waterways, considered 1952 to be the ultimate catastrophe, labeling it "the 100-year flood," although none of them had been here in the prior century. Comforted by their assessment, I assumed we wouldn't be seeing any more of that nonsense. I was born and raised in St. Paul and had never been aware of floods. Snow yes, even blizzards, but floods were not a concern. The closer I became associated with the old Miss, the more it seemed inclined to leave its banks.

In the fall of 1952 TCB had neither barges nor towboats, just high aspirations. The owners also managed the St. Paul Yacht Club. Its docks clung to the edge of TCB's rented property, the old Dingle Boat Works. We were building a 600 hp towboat on the ramshackle marine way left over from building several World War II sub chasers. It could launch but not lift vessels. My father, Paul, and a group of his friends had loaned money to TCB on the assurance that the towboat would profit from the burgeoning harbor traffic.

My dad had a sentimental attachment to the river because his father, Col. George Lambert, was a champion of the nine-foot-channel project and had been appointed to head the first St. Paul Port Authority. He was also an officer in the state militia, later the National Guard, and rose to be its head. My life and the colonel's overlapped only briefly, he having been taken by a heart attack in 1934.

A lawyer by trade, Grandpa Lambert and a handful of other visionaries from the Farmers Union had been so bold as to foster the improvement of the Upper Mississippi despite the opposition of some of the nation's railroad titans. Only the Depression and World War II had been powerful enough to override the objections of the railroads to the development of the Mississippi as a competing artery of commerce in the Midwest. The Colonel died before the nine-foot channel was completed, but in recognition of his efforts the city of St. Paul named the Jackson Street steamboat landing in his honor. Whether he looked down and smiled at my modest entry into the river business is debatable.

While the two existing officers (and only office staff) of TCB dithered about importantly, I threw myself into the business: running errands, decking, operating a tiny open work boat (the *Sea Mule* and an inboard launch, the *Missfit*), inspecting barges for damage, and even cleaning barges for change of cargo.

Cumbersome life jackets were in evidence, but no one wore them in those days, except at government locks. Life vests were apparently for sissies. (Nobody ever saw Mark Twain wearing a life jacket.) When I was in charge, I remedied that. The Mississippi and its current are unforgiving.

My efforts as a deckhand were determined but flawed. The towboat crewmen hooted at my initial attempts to tie manila lines, the real river rats terming my mooring technique, the "Buffalo City round hitch." I ended most days exhausted and dirty, but I was learning the business from the ground up, or was it from the water surface up?

As I took on more responsibilities, it became apparent that the rest of management was leaning on their oars, so the investors sought their departure. I was elevated to chief-in-charge of everything, at $50.00 per week. That was more than a tech sergeant's pay, except that Uncle Sam always paid and sometimes TCB didn't have the money. I took notes that were later traded for stock, and with my soldier's savings I became a major shareholder in this struggling enterprise.

That and my pending marriage to Dolly Carley drove me to excel. We had sales of about $250,000 my first year and recorded an almost identical loss. That was made possible by the prior management ignoring accounts payable and even collecting federal withholding taxes but not tendering them to the government. What a business! So, I had a considerable challenge, but with long hours and hard work it seemed surmountable. Ah, youth.

Among the legions of unforgettable characters that I was to encounter on the river, one of the most memorable came on the scene in that first year. Ernie Rieck and his towboat *Wabash* had been chartered to do the towing while TCB's new boat was taking shape. Ernie was ruggedly handsome and possessed a marvelous smile matched by an upbeat personality, a requisite when nearly everything went wrong. And for Ernie, Murphy's Law seemed constantly at work.

Ernie had gone to World War II from his native Chicago as a coxswain on a landing craft. When he returned home, he had a dream of using a towboat and hopper barges to bring salt from the Gulf Coast to his family hardware business. The Rieck family owned Grand Hardware on Chicago's South Side, near the Illinois Waterway. Ernie had hit several Pacific beaches under fire, so the prospect of barging salt from Avery Island to Chicago seemed a relatively simple task. He acquired a small 400 hp twin-screw towboat (and named it the *Wabash*) and a pair of old 175-by-26-foot hopper barges, then discovered that he had gotten the cart in front of the horse. First of all, the salt deposits just off the Louisiana coast were underwater, and secondly, someone else owned the mineral rights, a corporation named Cargill. Also, it proved cheaper to buy bulk salt and have it barged to Chicago than to employ Ernie's do-it-yourself scheme. Hence Grand Hardware and its subsidiary, Grand Salt, had to use their one boat in some other gainful service. That was where the needs of Ernie and TCB intersected. While waiting for the mv. (motor vessel) *St. Paul* to be launched and outfitted, TCB chartered the mv. *Wabash* "fully found," meaning, with crew.

It was a bit of a stretch to say the *Wabash* had a crew. Ernie was captain, mate, chief engineer and cook. The rest of the crew consisted of one square-built, bull-necked man with a rumpled face and a single eye. It was necessary to concentrate on the good eye, because your gaze was drawn to the gnarled hole in his face where the other eye should have been. No pretentious eye patch. Ugly-Eye was supposed to be deckhand and assistant engineer, but performed neither task when drunk or sleeping. His speech was sparse but colorful, mostly four-letter words. I don't recall any "argh matey," but it would not have been surprising. With his tattered, grease-stained clothes and the one eye, he resembled a pirate who had lost his cutlass. And since Ernie was no fashion plate, the pair frequently looked like they had just fallen off the same turnip wagon.

Ernie sailed from St. Paul on towing assignments that I gave him. That seemed simple enough, but it turned out to be like dispatching combat patrols into the jungle. The *Wabash* had no radio, and this was in the days just prior to radiotelephones.

For example, Ernie would leave St. Paul with orders to tow a barge load of fertilizer to Port Cargill on the Minnesota River and return with a loaded grain barge. The trip upstream should have taken three hours, four at the most. But as time passed, and I could no longer bear the frenzied calls from Cargill demanding to know where the hell their barge was, I would set out in search of the lost tow. Easier said than done.

The Minnesota River joined the Mississippi near Fort Snelling at Pike Island, so named after the explorer who invented Pike's Peak. Above there to Savage, the location of Port Cargill, the river traced a narrow corkscrew in a wide valley that had been scoured by receding floods ages ago. Between it's mouth and the Cargill terminal, some 14 miles to the southwest, there were only two road crossings and a few dead-end dirt roads along the densely wooded river banks. The Minnesota was not dredged as part of the nine-foot project until the mid-60s, so it was a challenge to navigate. During World War II a boatyard had been erected at Savage and several landing craft had been constructed there. Cargill subsequently acquired the site for a commodities terminal.

Ernie Rieck had never seen the Minnesota River until he took on the charter job for TCB, but gamely attacked the channel, which was dangerously low for most of the year. Once out of sight from a short river road in Mendota, he was lost in the jungle-like valley. If I couldn't spot him near Mendota, close by the mouth of the river, I had to proceed in a roundabout way to the next crossing. If he was still lost to view, I then repeated the process, leapfrogging to the next vantage point. Sometimes that worked and I caught a glimpse of Ernie's tow (or heard his diesels) and could estimate his arrival at his destination. But if he stranded somewhere on a sandbar between vantage points, it was like the Minnesota River Valley had swallowed him.

On one occasion he vanished as if space aliens had abducted him, Ugly-Eye, towboat and barge. None of my viewing sights yielded any clue to his location. In desperation, I set out on foot at random spots along the riverbank, battling my way through brush and swarming insects to probe those portions of the river that were only visible from God's perch.

After another sweaty trek, I was rewarded by the sound of idling diesel engines and finally caught sight of the *Wabash*. While flanking a tight bend in the river Ernie had swung the towboat too close to an overhanging cottonwood tree and a branch as thick as a man's thigh had impaled the pilot house through a side window. There sat Ernie, astride the offending timber, sawing his way toward freedom. From the engine room door Ugly-Eye offered an imbecilic wave, as if he had just been discovered on a Caribbean cruise. It was moments like this that prompted me to investigate the wonders of marine radios and radiotelephones.

On another occasion, I had to meet Ernie in Minneapolis with supplies and orders. It was a bright, beautiful fall day, and from several vantage points where Twin City parkways paralleled the great Mississippi gorge, I could easily see the *Wabash* with its coal barge, chugging toward its destination. Here above Lock and Dam 1 there would be no cottonwood encounters, no problems with shoaling in the calm waters of the upper pool. It promised to be an unexceptional voyage. What could go wrong?

I reached the terminal ahead of the tow and stood on the dock watching Ernie's approach. He spotted me and stepped from the pilothouse onto the bridge wing to flash his hearty smile and give me a big wave. Then he stepped back inside, and, about 400 feet from the dock wall, rang the engine room for reverse. The *Wabash* had no pilothouse controls, just the old system of signals to the engine room, where Ugly-Eye would throw the reverse levers. Nothing.

Ernie stepped out on the bridge wing again, and I could hear him bellow something down toward the engine room. He gave me another quick wave, his smile a bit less effusive, and stepped back into the pilothouse, thrashing the reverse signal. Still nothing happened to slack the speed of the oncoming tow.

With the bow of the coal barge now just 100 feet from the dock, Ernie cast aside his optimism, dashed from the pilothouse down two ladders and into the engine room. The engines reversed, belching black smoke, but too late to kill the inexorable forward motion of the barge and its 1,300 tons of coal. As I watched helplessly, the tow caromed off the sheet piling dock on its pilotless passage toward St. Anthony Falls. Ugly-Eye had apparently been napping among the diesels.

Ernie did an Olympic sprint up both ladders back to the pilothouse. By this point he was about even with me, and I got another wave and a smile as he yelled, "Everything's OK!"

The tow began to lose headway, and Ugly-Eye peered out of the engine room with as angelic a look as an inebriated pirate could muster. Disaster had been deferred to another day.

It came late in the fall at Pike Island. Ernie was towing a salt load to Port Cargill and had just entered the mouth of the Minnesota River when the barge hit bottom and came to a stop. It was that dry season when the river was at flat pool and the shoals began to assert themselves, especially on the Minnesota. The accepted method of freeing a grounded barge was to reverse engines full and attempt to flush out the bar under the barge. Ernie commenced this maneuver with the stern of the *Wabash* alongside Pike Island. After several minutes of high-powered flushing, the island bank began to erode and an aged tree was undermined. It came crashing down across the stern gunwale of the *Wabash* and threatened to sink it.

By the grace of God, or the Mobil Oil Co., the mv. *La Crosse*

Socony happened to be passing the mouth of the Minnesota River, and its crew witnessed the unfolding disaster. They got a line on the tree and backed it off the *Wabash* in the nick of time. When Ernie departed St. Paul for Chicago in November, still smiling, his poor old towboat had a permanent crimp across the stern gunwales from it final encounter with the Minnesota River.

My first year in the river industry had been a crash course in near catastrophe and the beginning of my exposure to a variety of saints and sinners. What a voyage I had embarked upon!

CHAPTER 2

BRANCHING OUT

In 1953 TCB launched the mv. *St. Paul*, thanks to another flood that eased it off the marine ways that no longer functioned. This spring's high water lacked the drama of a 100-year flood, but it still soaked the old office in the Dingle Boat Works. Enough already! We acquired an old wooden barge and equipped it with a Quonset hut and a sump pump. I reckoned myself to be a jump ahead of nature and its ability to disrupt my administration of TCB.

By the start of the navigation season we finally had the mv. *St. Paul* running — well, after a fashion. Gordy Miller, TCB's founder, had decided to be an engineering pioneer designing the machinery on the new towboat. Having never heard the adage that what the pioneers got for their trouble were a lot of arrows in their behinds, Gordy had designed a rarity: a triple-screw towboat. That in itself was somewhat revolutionary for its day, but instead of installing the tried and true General Motors 6-71 engines that had proven themselves on thousands of World War II craft, he selected the new 220 hp GM 6-110 diesels. The mv. *St. Paul* had about a 10-year shakedown cruise. I learned that the primary advantage of three engines was that you could still do some towing with two, because one was always down for repairs. It was triple trouble.

What I knew about diesels was nil, and Gordy Miller knew only slightly more. But barge traffic into the Twin Cities was still light, only about 2.5 million tons annually, and with a limited season we had time for tinkering with the "Gimmys."

❖❖❖

Winter generally arrives in Minnesota like the meteor that wiped out the dinosaurs. It brings a battery-cracking, tire-squaring cold that causes water temperatures to plummet, and despite river current, ice begins to form. If the thermometer should fall below zero, as it can even in November, that ice will generally remain for the winter. It can be broken downward by a towboat, but sheets of ice, with massive lateral density, cannot be pushed aside easily, and it paves the wider reaches of the river like Lake Pepin, halting barge traffic on the Upper Mississippi. There is no reprieve from nature's sentence. You can almost bet on ice-making weather about the last week in November, and for the next four months it only gets worse. The arrival of winter and river ice always coincides with the harvest of corn, wheat and soybeans in a diabolical way. Just when the demand for shipping grain reaches its peak, the weather conspires to present river men with the worst operating conditions.

When the river reopens for barge traffic in the spring, we call it "the season," as if we were in the resort business. The arrival of the first tow through Lake Pepin, near April 1, is cause for short-lived jubilation. We had paying customers again. But that was followed in a few weeks by the spring runoff. You could almost set your watch by the flood crest. It came with astounding regularity about April 15th, and the high water hung around for one to two weeks, interrupting our season.

What a business model, eight months of revenue activity and

sometimes just seven. The navigation season was preceded by a generally destructive flood and ended with ice breaking.

The winter doldrums, while without revenue, were partly necessary for us to overhaul equipment and patch hulls under the supervision of Al Beck, a portly, jovial Swede who was our port engineer. Al was one of those mechanical geniuses who could repair your wristwatch or your diesel engine, and disassembled either without any reservation.

In addition to using the off season for towboat maintenance and repair, I used the next one to marry Dolly Carley. And she began sharing my years of frenetic life in the river business. She was no June bride. June was the navigation season. We wed in mid-February, to the amusement of her family.

In 1954 we also began a volatile relationship with Frank Aiple, a self-made river man from Stillwater, Minn., on the banks of the St. Croix. Frank was a born mechanic who loved to tinker with heavy equipment. He acquired a war surplus landing craft, filled it with used diesels and brought it to Stillwater. There he set about building towboats, some of the ugliest ever seen on the Mississippi. He ultimately lopped the bow and stern off the landing craft, turning it into a dry dock.

We made the mistake of chartering two of Frank's do-it-yourself creations, the 500 hp mv. *Cree* and the 250 hp mv. *Tom Thumb*. The charter fees for two years nearly had us on the financial ropes, because the old Cummings engines in these boats would only function properly when Frank or his chief mechanic was there to mother them. I was trying to run a harbor towing business and had little patience with the continuous breakdowns. Frank and I clashed repeatedly. He had the flexibility of a rusted lug nut, and I wasn't inclined to back off either. A couple of lawsuits and a settlement terminated our use of his towboats and put him into the harbor business as a competitor about 1957.

There were memorable moments with those towboats, particularly the little two-deck *Tom Thumb*. We employed a number of river rats from Prescott and Pepin, Wis. One of them, John Biles, piloted the single-screw *Tom Thumb*, which was considered a Jonah by the other boat crews. Indeed there wasn't much to the tiny boat. It had one deck with a square pilothouse on top resembling an outdoor privy. A set of controls extended through the roof of the pilothouse, so that John could stand on top in the open and see over empty barges. He did this with a certain panache, but the visual challenges frequently caused him to hit the bank on the winding Minnesota River.

There was one particular hairpin bend on the Minnesota where an old lady lived in a ramshackle house. John hit the bank there frequently, causing chunks to fall in the water and incurring the wrath of the resident. She took to throwing things at John when he got too close. The missile might be a clod of dirt, a stone or a tomato. John named that spot "Mad Woman Bend." There was another dogleg on the Minnesota that frequently caused groundings: "Dredge Cut," just below Cargill. It was later eliminated when the Corps of Engineers assumed responsibility for the Minnesota. The well-dredged Mississippi River also had its waterloo for pilots at "Monkey Rudder Bend," in the narrows just below Lock and Dam 1.

One of the worst spots to negotiate on the Minnesota River was just under the Mendota Bridge. This highway bridge is high, running from bluff to bluff, but just under it snaked the Minneapolis, Northfield & Southern (MN&S) Railroad Bridge, a swing bridge in a beastly curve of the river. John Biles was down bound one spring day with a loaded grain barge in some substantial current. While attempting to flank the bend, he hit the Pike Island pier of the MN&S with some 1,800 tons of steel and grain.

"Just hit it a glancing blow," John said.

The decades-old pier made of wooden piles covered with rock and masonry had been moved about a foot — not something that could be readily patched.

We were horrified that we might have to buy a new pier for the MN&S, but Chicago admiralty attorney, Edwin B. Hayes, found a flaw in their aged construction permit, and since the railroad was already considering abandoning the branch line, we avoided a calamitous lawsuit. John Biles wanted to paint a bridge pier on the side of his pilothouse and suggested that five such marks would make him an ace.

◈ ◈ ◈

The departure of the St. Paul Yacht Club and their conglomeration of rickety docks and bitching, tool-borrowing, bad-credit boaters cleared the way for a focus on the commercial towing business. Gordy Miller left TCB to be harbor master at the Yacht Club, making both of us happy.

It was obvious that I could no longer direct the towing operations without radio communication, and we made that technological leap, which meant fewer forays into the jungle of the Minnesota River bottoms for me. I also began to hear the other river traffic and came to enjoy the pilot-to-pilot conversations, particularly the dialects. Capt. Louis Nyhammer, of the *La Crosse Socony*, spoke in his lilting Scandinavian to the Bayou Fleet, its captains responding in their Cajun drawl.

One day I made repeated calls on the radio trying to locate an approaching line-haul towboat. No answer. Then my phone rang and the voice on the other end said, "They're in Lock 3 right now, Jack."

I was pretty certain that it wasn't God. Hugh MacMillan, part of the Cargill family, was a ham radio operator and apparently monitored the marine channel.

◇◇◇

The pride of our fleet, the mv. *St. Paul*, arrived one day with an underside problem instead of the usual GM difficulty. Something had jammed a propeller and rudder on one side. Without a dry dock, we were reluctant to do anything until we could determine the cause. A call went out for commercial diver Carl Gause and son. While we awaited the hard-hat diver, Gladys Kuhn, the matronly cook on the mv. *St. Paul* (and known as "Happy Bottom" as are all riverboat ladies named Gladys), went into the office for a chat. On her return to the towboat lying alongside the office barge, she made a misstep and went down feet first off the stern. As she bobbed to the surface, Frannie Bilderback, a yard engineer, was right there to grab her and boost her back on the boat. It took about an hour for Gladys to put on some dry clothes and regain her composure, but she was otherwise unhurt.

A formidable talker, Gladys was soon blathering on about her dunking and how she could not imagine how that had happened, and how she had expected to meet her creator.

When she stopped for a breath my dad asked, "Gladys, did you happen to check the rudders while you were down there?"

She hadn't, so we were left to rely on the divers to find and remove a deadhead (a tree trunk) jammed between a screw and a backing rudder.

When a similar problem occurred again later with the mv. *St. Paul*, I was so concerned with the cost of the divers that I decided to conduct an inspection myself. Besides, Gladys Kuhn remained adamant about not doing an underwater check. It was not one of my more rational decisions. With a rope attached to my waist and being held by Al Beck, I slid under the stern of the towboat to see what I could see. Even at near flat-pool stage I learned what should have been obvious from the surface. Because of a constant load of suspended solids, you can't see six inches in front of your face in the Mississippi River channel. I was unable to make any judgment and got a couple of bumps on the head from the underside of the boat for my trouble. Imagine! I now had a responsible job, a wife and a child on the way.

We ended up summoning the divers anyway, who helped the yard crew replace a damaged rudder.

My cousin, Dick Lambert, later tried the "rope-around-the-waist" diving trick with no better result. The Mississippi was clear as mud.

◈ ◈ ◈

River men from the Wisconsin side of the Mississippi dominated the ranks of our towboat and shipyard crews. Prescott gave us Pert Perdue and Popeye Tronier, and five Schickling brothers, many of whom worked for us at various times. All of the Schicklings were accomplished river pilots, and Whitey eventually became our marine superintendent. From Pepin came Bill Lawson, Jim Fleming, the Biles brothers and others. From St. Paul we enlisted Roy Wethern, a veteran steamboat pilot who had a short run with us, and Don Wright, who had operated work boats in Greenland for the government. Don eventually became our port captain.

◇◇◇

As waterway traffic slowly expanded the river carriers began asking us to perform rudimentary barge repairs, and our own modest maintenance staff of three swelled to near 300 by the 1970s, when we went into hopper-barge fabrication. But that was some 20 years in the future. In the late 1950s we were just trying to keep old pre-World War II barges afloat. Federal Barge Line had a conglomeration of hulks, some of riveted construction and others made during the war when steel was precious and hulls were thin. I tried my hand at welding, but Al Beck said my cuts held better than my welds.

As chief (and only) barge inspector for TCB, I searched for cracks and damaged barge covers and then assigned repair crews to fix them. Lacking a dry dock, we could only undertake topside work, but on occasion we would have a towboat ram a barge onto a nearby beach and expose the bow or a knuckle for welding. I wondered if that was the way the ancients had done it on the Nile.

These repairs also involved the brutal chore of getting pumps to crippled barges that had not previously disclosed an injury, or to loaded barges that arrived in town leaking. The line-haul towboat crews were notorious for caulking a crack made by hitting a submerged wing dam, then telling us that we might want to check a certain FBL barge as it might have a teensy leak. The "small leak" often turned out to be a tear that resembled a torpedo hit. It had been pumped and caulked with a bundle of shingles by the line-haul towboat crew, just good enough to hold until boat and crew could get out of town. Then the shingles let go, usually at night or on a weekend, and we had a sinking coal barge in our fleet landing. Getting Homelite pumps onto these sinkers was a way of doctoring them until they could be unloaded and the crack welded from the outside. Some of the old Federal barges had so many patches they resembled war orphans.

Because the calls of alarm regarding sinkers came at odd hours, I was frequently the one to wrestle the Homelite pump into a truck (or a trunk) and get it across a dock at terminals like Farmers Union or Northern States Power. And the pending disasters to both boats and barges took no holidays. Indeed, while the river flowed, the towboats towed.

This sort of crisis work was arduous, but a twenty-something-year-old thinks he is invincible. Don Seiford and Dick Nitti, a couple of local boys, eventually took over the barge inspection and repair business, but not before I injured a lower lumbar disk and had to admit to some physical limitations.

Part of the early barge repair team included a war veteran named Chuck Lund, who had a prosthetic device where he had lost his left hand. He was an artist with welding gear but once lost his concentration and welded his hook to a barge deck.

To differentiate it from the towing operation, we grandly called the repair service Twin City Shipyard.

◇◇◇

Still another facet of our business conglomerate was "fleeting." By renting idle shoreline from the Port Authority we provided barge parking lots for the carriers, which were called fleets. Incoming or outgoing barges were secured at these locations. It was not as simple as auto parking. The barges were moored to shore by cables. Regardless of circumstances, TCB was responsible for those moored barges. And an empty jumbo (195-by-35-foot) barge weighed over 300 tons. When loaded, the barge and cargo approximated 1,700 tons. Half a dozen loaded barges adrift on the river currents presented an irresistible force, taking out barge terminals or bridges. And when those barges came loose, like cattle getting through the fence, it was our responsibility. Since our harbor boats weren't always available in such emergencies, we employed night watchmen to guard against breakaways. These breakaway mini-disasters always seemed to come at night.

One of our night watchmen was a teen named Nick Steckhan. (Called "Steckhan the Deckhand" by boat crews.) He had come from a somewhat troubled background and had a bad stutter, but he was a good kid and begged for a job of some kind. One night while making his watchman rounds, Nick spotted some barges drifting above our wharf barge. He called me in a state of high anxiety and said, "B…B…Barges loooose."

I tried to calm him down, but I needed to assess the gravity of the situation. So I told him to go back, look upstream for a minute and see if he could get a count.

He came back on the phone presently and said, "There are f… f…four of the b…b…bastards."

Luckily, it was not a period of flood currents. I got on the radio-telephone and summoned the nearest towboat to corral the critters. A year or two later Nick joined the Navy. When he came back to visit us, his stutter was completely gone. Had he stayed in the river business he probably would have become a nervous wreck.

CHAPTER 3
PERILS OF THE RIVER

In the post-war years, the infant barge industry was still dominated by the government's Inland Waterways Corporation (IWC), otherwise known as the Federal Barge Lines. The Interstate Commerce Commission bestowed limited common-carrier rights, and rates for certain non-bulk commodities were tightly regulated. Only bulk freight, such as coal, grain and petroleum, were unregulated.

Federal Barge Lines (FBL) had an array of barges of various sizes and some ponderously big towboats, many of which had been converted from steam to diesel. Along with FBL, Mississippi Valley Barge Line, American Barge Line, Mechling Barge Line, Ohio River Company and John I. Hay were the prime carriers of regulated freight and dry bulk cargo. The primary non-regulated liquid carriers were Commercial Barge Line, Canal Barge Line, Ingram Barge Co., Upper Mississippi Towing Corp., Brent Towing and National Marine Service. Although many lines were family businesses begun by river men with one towboat, the flow of commerce in the 1950s was structured and well ordered, based on the restrictions to entry and the high capital cost associated with river equipment. This structure would expand steadily then wither and almost vanish within 30 years.

The principal common carriers had agents in major communities, and the IWC had wharf barges in many of those locations. These were large deck barges with warehouse-type metal sheds moored at terminals in major port areas. The IWC divested itself of the terminals and the wharf barges shortly after World War II, selling the facilities to private warehousing firms or local port authorities. As the package freight trade declined, the wharf barges became obsolete for terminal operations and TCB managed to acquire the one in St. Paul via a long-term lease with the St. Paul Port Authority.

This acquisition of the mammoth riveted-hull wharf barge allowed TCB to stop clinging to the bank or its tiny office barge. It gave us a base of towing operations, a supply point and a machine shop, all moored on the channel. The facility also freed us from the floods that plagued the old shore-based Dingle yard. What we had not counted on was fire. A heater on the wharf barge caused a fire one winter that destroyed the shed and most of its contents. The barge was untouched, so we built a new shed. I had experienced floods and now a fire. What was next, I wondered, a plague of locusts? That next spring came close. It was one of the worst ever on the river for mayflies.

While visiting our local insurance agent regarding the wharf barge fire and standing in his outer office chatting about our string of bad luck, another client listened somewhat incredulously and asked, "How do you have a flood?"

I replied that I just had a knack for it.

Of the major waterway carriers, Federal (acquired by the owner of St. Louis Ship) and Mississippi Valley Barge Line (called simply, the Valley Line by one and all) had agents in the Twin Cities.

Federal had a series of local agents, including Bob Streckfus, of the Streckfus Steamer clan. Bob, a pilot by trade, worked at FBL because there were not enough top slots in the family business. One day I was taking him to inspect some FBL barges on our little work boat, the *Sea Mule*. As I was rounding what I knew from experience was a shallow spot near the fleet, which I had intended to avoid, Bob seemed to think that I was making an amateurish turn at slow speed and confidently insisted that he, a licensed captain, take the helm for the landing. I stepped aside and let him run the *Sea Mule* aground. It provided a moment of minor satisfaction from a riverboat captain who, like many of them, held a superior opinion of himself. They believed in that Mark Twain line about river pilots being some of God's chosen. And at times, in high current and during downstream landings or lockings, they deserved such accolades.

The Valley Line soon appointed James C. O'Brien to be their agent in the Twin Cities. He was a courtly gentleman from McComb, Miss., who served a long tour of duty at the head of navigation. A bachelor, Jimmy was extraordinarily polite and a pleasure to have around. He danced with all the wives at Propeller Club parties and went out of his way to remember the names of everyone's kids. His only known fault was that he drove every place without exceeding 35 miles per hour. He could take an hour to drive from Minneapolis to St. Paul. When Valley Line executives came to town they soon learned that they could accomplish more if they rented a car. Virgil Angel, Valley's traffic manager, once told me that he had to restrain himself from jumping out and running ahead of Jimmy's car.

While I was getting my advanced education in the College of Mississippi River Hard Knocks, Bob Maher my buddy from high school and the Air Force, as well as my best man, got his four-year degree at St. Thomas College. Jobs were not all that plentiful, and having observed the thrill-a-minute pace at TCB, he decided to join up with me once more. We split the administrative chores and the dispatching, each doing the latter day and night for a month at a stretch. We also became shirttail relations when Bob wed Dolly's sister, Betty Lou. They, likewise, planned their wedding so as not to interfere with the navigation season.

TCB affairs almost derailed Bob and Betty Lou's wedding. Along with Bob and my dad, I had driven down to Lake Pepin to see where the first towboat of the season was, as it made its way through the ice. As fate would have it, the tow was not anywhere in sight. So we drove on a bit farther and then a little farther, sure that we would spot that first tow just round the next bend. We finally caught up with it at about Winona. Then we stopped for lunch and a noon nip or two.

By the time we got Bob back to his house, it was past suppertime. The problem was that his family, his fiancée and her parents were meeting there for the first time. There were a few frosty moments while Bob explained that this was important business, not just a junket. He was a smooth talker and managed to keep the wedding on track despite the bad company he had kept that day.

◇◇◇

As river traffic volume edged slowly upward, the carriers began to call on us for more services. In addition to barge fleeting and repairs, we started providing basic ship chandlery items, rope, cable, fuel and lubricating oil. We would even order groceries for towboat crews, although finding chicory coffee for the Deep South crews proved a challenge on the tundra.

There were other, even more extraordinary requests. One Sunday morning I was asked to locate a pump impeller for the Valley Line's mv. *Tennessee*. The item was no bigger than my fist, but its failure in the circulating system on the mighty ex-steamer had stranded it while southbound in Lake Pepin near Stockholm, Wis.

This was the era when businessmen believed in service, so the owner of the small company that provided such "once in a blue moon" items met me at his shop to supply the $20.00 rubber impeller. With four-year-old Danny as my navigator (Dolly having stayed home with his new baby sister, Paula) we headed down the picturesque Wisconsin side of the Mississippi, like the cavalry to the rescue.

The big towboat and its tow of some dozen barges was moored well off the channel, up against the shore right at picturesque Stockholm. The natives were used to seeing river tows, but never one almost ashore just off Main Street, and the entire town had gathered to view the acres of steel that had beached in their quiet village.

Fortunately, the *Tennessee* had an empty coal barge or two spiked out on the head of the tow, and one of them hovered above the bank. When I arrived, they lowered a ladder and the PA system boomed, "Come aboard, while we fix the pump!"

Danny got on my back and hung on around my neck while I climbed the ladder. It was an exercise that would have horrified the womenfolk in our family, but it drew cheers from the Wisconsin Cheese Heads, who had not often witnessed such heroics in tiny Stockholm. Danny climbed all the ships ladders to the pilothouse, where he was allowed to sit in the captain's chair and play that he was "driving." The captain even held him up for a pull or two on the whistle cord. The experience may have planted an early seed for

Dan's eventual naval career.

We were then plied with pie a la mode and other goodies by the ship's cook, a grandmother too far from her own kids, until the engineer announced that the pump was repaired. Danny and I clambered back down the ladder, and the mighty mv. *Tennessee* headed south, giving the Stockholm crowd several triumphant air-horn blasts.

◈ ◈ ◈

Right behind some modest expansion of TCB business activity the unions arrived. We got two of them before you could say, "Monkey Rudder Bend." The good folks from Prescott helped usher in the Masters, Mates and Pilots Union, followed closely by the National Maritime Union for all crew beneath the Texas deck. We resisted the latter unionization, based on our "close" relations with the younger deck and galley crew, triggering a National Labor Relations Board election. Several crew members sidled up to me to whisper that they had voted for the company. I felt reassured but learned another lesson when the results were tallied. It was 18 to 0 for the NMU. Never trust anyone but your mother.

Our relations with the unions suffered the normal ups and downs, and the union representatives were even helpful on occasion. We negotiated hard at contract time and even went to the brink of a strike several times, but the guys from the major carriers, who always accused us of charging too much for harbor switching, were the first ones to blink and insist that we had to settle. The Valley Line, etc., could not afford a strike at the upper end of the Upper.

Contract negotiations were usually grinding affairs, akin to root canal surgery without the Novocain, but they had their moments of levity. Charlie Jones, of the MMP, was pleading for an extra paid holiday, "Easter Day," he called it. Bob Maher suggested that the contract reflect "Easter Sunday" as it usually fell on that day of the week.

Soon the local chapter of the operating engineers union represented the shipyard employees.

◈ ◈ ◈

We were not the only harbor operators in the Twin City area. The curmudgeonly Harry Harris and his son Harry Jr. operated the mv. *Harry Harris*. By the late 1950s the local sand, gravel and ready-mix supplier, the J. L. Shiely Co., began to mine aggregate from Grey Cloud Island, south of St. Paul, and barged it to yards in St. Paul and Minneapolis. Another pair of Prescott natives, the Beeler brothers, piloted Shiely's towboat. One of the brothers soon added a chapter to local river lore.

A beautiful little Luscombe Silvaire on floats had just landed near the Holman Field seaplane dock when it received a puncture in one float from what was likely a "propeller inspector" (an upside down tree). Before the pilot could taxi to the seaplane landing, the plane began to list heavily on the damaged float and started to turn turtle in the river channel near our office. One of our yard-work boats rescued the pilot and passenger just as the plane flipped upside down. We alerted the airport staff and radioed our towboats to steer clear of the delicate derelict until we could corral it.

Then along came Shiely's towboat, the mv. *Joealjim* (named for three Shiely brothers). One of the Beeler's, without the slightest hesitation, faced up to an upside-down pontoon and pushed the Luscombe out of the channel, grinding it into the bottom near the airport. A careful salvage operation and subsequent reconditioning might have saved the aluminum beauty, but after the Beeler tow job

26

it resembled a squashed beer can. I suggested to Bob Shiely that they paint a small airplane on the side of the pilothouse to represent their "kill."

For once we had been associated with a disaster that would not have to be explained to our insurance agent. But that Old Man River never relents in its efforts to humble and defeat. I was flying to Chicago early one morning, and as the Northwest flight rose eastbound I followed our course down the river noting towboats and barges along the way. Passing downtown St. Paul, I spotted our office barge for a few brief seconds. Funny thing, it looked lopsided. Must have been an optical illusion, I mused. After landing at O'Hare I called the office. No answer. I called Dolly, and she confirmed that the sump pump had failed and the office barge had settled to the bottom.

We salvaged what office equipment we could, but what a mess it was! This provided an unexpected opportunity for us to move to a real office on dry land in the largely vacant administration building at nearby Holman Field. It was just a chip shot from the yard and the wharf barge. We were even on the second floor, high above the Mississippi. It seemed that we had outmaneuvered Old Man River. But he was just biding his time and would return with another surge that made the prior floods look like garden parties.

CHAPTER 4
THAT TODDLIN' TOWN

The struggle to make a consistent profit from the harbor towing business had been frustrated by the limitations of the Upper Mississippi navigation season. So when an opportunity was presented for us to get into the harbor towing business in Chicago, we jumped at the chance. As it turned out, we jumped into the deep end of the pool. Winter also comes to Chicago, but except for a few weeks of occasional ice, the Illinois River was open to navigation most of the year. And in that flat land next to Lake Michigan, there was no flood season.

George Hales had owned Chicago Towing Co. When he died suddenly in 1961, his son Ken set out to sell the business. Chicago Towing owned just two small towboats and a couple of worn tank barges and had no permanent base in the complex Chicago river-and-canal system. They had several competitors, including the formidable aggregate giant, Material Service Co.; Hannah Towing Co., primarily a petroleum carrier; and a couple of Calumet-area tug operators. Great Lakes Towing Co., part of the Material Service empire, was also present but focused on handling sea-going ships.

When I broached the subject of financing the acquisition of Chicago Towing, the officers of our staid Empire Bank of St. Paul were aghast. I might as well have been trying to fund an opium den alongside the cathedral. Already uneasy about lending money to us for Twin City river operations, they told us to leave and never again darken their hallowed halls. (I later learned that my uncle Dan Hickey, a prominent St. Paul businessman, had guaranteed our first loan with the Empire. Those guys were real gamblers.) However, the Pullman Bank of South Chicago had financed Chicago Towing, and that enterprising group of bankers agreed to finance both our Twin City- and Chicago-based assets. There in 1961 we began a wonderful relationship with Don O'Toole, Jim Grell and Bruno Valente of the Pullman. That turned out to be the easy part of getting established in Chicago.

When we actually began to operate, we encountered an organization and cast of characters that seemed to have stepped out of a movie. A union called the Licensed Tugmens' Protective Association, headed by a rotund gent named Patty Cullinan, put out pickets in a rowboat wherever we handled barges, causing both the terminals and the barge lines to shun our services. We were already unionized, and our two unions, the MMP and the NMU, already had crews aboard our towboats in keeping with our contractual obligations. It mattered not to the glowering Patty Cullinan. He just wanted us to go away. He even set up a picket line at the Pullman Bank, brandishing a sign that said Pullman had loaned money to a scab outfit.

We went into district court to seek the removal of the pickets, but the judge, who was reluctant to judge, bucked the matter off to the National Labor Relations Board. At a meeting before the NLRB the hearing officer dismissed the matter as beyond NLRB jurisdiction, because the pilots on our boats were supervisors. After an agonizing week or two, we got the matter before Superior

Court in Cook County. The Tugmens' attorney argued that because TCB was involved in interstate commerce, it was a federal matter beyond that court's jurisdiction. A feisty old judge ruled from the bench that since we were already unionized and our employees had already made their choice of AFL-CIO unions, this was not a labor-management issue, and since we had already been before a federal agency (the NLRB), we were entitled to justice somewhere in the land, therefore he was going to stop the merry-go-round of legal gymnastics. He ordered the Tugmen to cease and desist its harassment of TCB, its employees and its customers. That night I got drunk with my bankers and lawyers.

We established an operating base in the Lemont area and set up shop there with Ray Rauch, formerly of Mid Continent Barge Line, as our manager. During my efforts to find this base I had occasion to canvas the Sanitary District shoreline and ran across my old friend, Ernie Rieck. He had acquired a lease on a piece of the waterfront near the family hardware business and was planning to build a warehouse for river freight. He also rented space to a few pleasure-boat owners. His two barges, allowed to settle along the shore, formed the "dock" of this diverse enterprise, and the old towboat *Wabash* was also shoring up the bank, partially flooded and heeled over about 20 degrees.

"Just have to pump her out, and she'll be ready to go," Ernie assured me.

His office was in an ancient house trailer guarded by a small drooping puppy that was secured outside with a piece of one-inch hawser.

Ernie eventually got his terminal building finished but apparently lacked talent in the application of the roof. A strong wind

30

came along one day and deposited most of the roof on adjacent railroad tracks. One of my people happened by as a frantic Ernie, dragging wreckage said, "C'mon and help me, the Illinois Central has a train through here in 30 minutes."

Despite his bad luck, Ernie survived to make a few bucks and splurged on a pink Cadillac convertible. The police, assuming that the disheveled old pirate must have "jacked" the car, frequently stopped him.

◇◇◇

The Pullman Bank was like a breath of fresh air compared to the stodgy St. Paul bankers. They not only made an attempt to understand the river business but were aggressive in lending. We banked with them for the better part of 20 years, until TCB outgrew their loan capacity. Another benefit turned out to be the great individuals at the Pullman. Jim Grell and Bruno Valente became good friends, frequently visited us in St. Paul and even became duck hunting buddies.

Valente had a particularly creative sense of humor. When we took him to St. Paul City Hall to buy his non-resident duck hunting permit, he just about brought the house down. A dull clerk filling out the appropriate forms asked Bruno if he would be hunting on Indian reservation land. It would cost an extra $10. The Chicago banker hesitated for just a few seconds, rolled his eyes then said, "You mean for another ten I can shoot an Indian?"

Grell, Maher and I were convulsed with laughter while the clerk gave us all her best Mother Superior frown. That made it all the funnier.

◇◇◇

The 50s and 60s had proved to be momentous years for TCB.

One of my most memorable personal events had been as an invited guest on board the sea-going yacht *Carmac*, the pride of the Cargill family. (It may have been the *Carmac I*. The *Carmac VII* would ultimately serve this wonderful family.) Normally berthed in Florida, the ship had made its one and only trek to Minneapolis, and how the deep-draft vessel had managed to get over the many lock sills is still a mystery to me. She was as long and slender as a Navy destroyer, near 150 feet, and had to have a draft exceeding nine feet.

On the brief visit to the homeland of the owners, she had cruised with many distinguished guests. And one night the fraternity of river rats (barge-line types) were invited aboard, courtesy of Don Brandenberg, VP of the company barge line, Cargo Carriers, Inc. After an inspection tour and cocktails, we were seated in the salon for a sumptuous meal served by a wait staff in white dinner jackets. The great oak dinning table must have been built in pieces and reassembled onboard. It was long and narrow, like the ship that surrounded it, and could not have been designed for any room other than that salon. The many chairs were of matching oak with high throne-like backs. It gave one the feeling of being in a "Knights of the Round Table" scene, except that the table was about 20 feet long. One could barely see people at either end.

It was a stag event and properly lubricated with before-, during- and after-dinner spirits. We were quietly contemplating our cigars when a thunderous crack sounded, as if the keel had been severed. None of us brave river men wanted to appear like sissies, but we all looked toward shore to see if we were still afloat and/or taking on a list. Then we noted that one of our number, Minor Hendrickson, of Federal Barge Line, was sinking slowly from sight as if shot. The base of his chair had broken where the legs met the chair back, and that towering back was pushing him down. He couldn't do anything but hang onto the table.

As soon as we realized that Minor was the only casualty, people next to him and waiters extracted him from beneath the great table. It was a howlingly funny event for everyone, although I am probably the only one alive to remember it — Hendrickson and the others having mostly gone to their rewards.

CHAPTER 5
AGAIN, THE 100-YEAR FLOOD

D espite competition in both the Twin City area and Chicago our business grew and prospered modestly. In 1957 my cousin Dick Lambert joined us, and later my brother Bill came on board.

The water transport industry expanded dramatically from 1960 to 1980. At times we had as many as 500 barges in the Twin City harbor, some 400 of which were our responsibility. We kept track of the armada on a huge plywood scheduling board that had first been erected in the Quonset hut office and transferred to several later offices. That board represented the complex harbor system from Pine Bend through St. Paul to Minneapolis and up the Minnesota River. Each barge was a numbered tag hooked somewhere on the map. At night the duty dispatcher took home a reasonable facsimile of the massive complex on a clipboard. Our process seems antiquated now, but Al Gore had not yet invented the personal computer.

Eventually the lower 14 miles of the Minnesota River were dredged by the Corps of Engineers, removing a couple of hairpin sections and forever eliminating conflict with the Lady of Madwoman Bend. When Northern States Power Co. added a coal-fired power plant at Bayport, Minn., on the St. Croix River, the overall harbor complex became nearly 100 miles in length.

To keep pace with increasing barge traffic, we added to our fleet of harbor towboats, acquiring used vessels as well as building our own. The most interesting of the old boats was perhaps the mv. *Hugh Blaske*, named for the patriarch of that great Alton, Ill.-based river family. She was powered by giant Fairbanks-Morse diesel engines that had to be started with a near explosion. Mechanic Frannie Bilderback became famous for his 4th of July effort to get the old engines firing. Someone described it as similar to Marryin' Sam's "$2 Wedding" of Al Capp cartoon fame.

Twin City Shipyard also manufactured new towboats, including the mv. *Paul H. Lambert*. Named for my dad and christened by my daughter Paula and my mother, Mary, the twin-screw vessel joined the fleet in 1965. It had a retractable pilothouse, which facilitated its operation in either the Twin City area or Chicago. Fortunately it was almost complete in the old shipyard building when the flood of 1965 was used as a launching tool. It was the only benefit to be derived from that spring flood.

◈◈◈

April of 1965 proved to be the 100-year flood — part deux. The high water not only swamped the old shipyard but spread onto the airport and up the steps of the Holman Field Administration building and into the first floor lobby. Thanks to my foresight, our new offices were on the second floor — an unusable island in a murky sea of roiling Mississippi. A handful of us repaired to the basement of my home to conduct business operations, such as they were. Little Scotty, our third child, was thrilled to have all the new playmates and expressed his enthusiasm by presenting one of the office ladies with a juicy angleworm.

The crest came on Sunday, April 16, and was much anticipated by the Twin City Barge family and the community at large. I happened to be passing through downtown St. Paul that day and noticed a throng on the Wabasha Street Bridge. Fearful that some maritime disaster was pending, I joined the crowd to look out on the bank-to-bank waters.

"What is everyone looking at?" I asked the nearest native.

"We're watching for the crest," he replied.

Despite the frequency of recent floods, the good people of St. Paul struggled with the difference between "crest" and "tidal wave."

We kept two towboats crewed and ready to move, as our wharf barge and a small fleet of cargo barges clung precariously to the riverbank north of the airport. A breakaway could have been disastrous because of the intense current. We had sent The mv. *St. Paul* to scout above the Robert Street Bridge, and the flow was so swift in those narrows that the 660 hp boat was halted and backed down. The actual peak flow, as measured by the Corps of Engineers at that point, was a dangerous 171,000 cubic feet per second. The Corps would routinely close Lock 1 to traffic when the flow there reached 30,000 cfs.

I was prompted to fulminate about the historic flood frequency to my friend Lee Hauser, chief of operations at the St. Paul office of the Corps of Engineers. "How the hell can this be? I'm experiencing a second 100-year flood."

"It's highly technical," he responded, "but what we now have is the 100-year flood about every 15 years."

Indeed the 1965 flood caused a decade-long flurry of flood plain abandonment and dike construction. Secondarily, it put TCB out of business for a month. The eight-month season was shortened to seven as the crest rolled down toward St. Louis, closing lock-and-dam facilities as it spread along 600 miles of the Upper Mississippi basin. What a business.

◈◈◈

Our grand corporate scheme was to standardize most of our harbor towboats so that they could operate in either St. Paul or Chicago. Bridges in the Windy City flatland area were universally low, with clearance only suitable for towboats with retractable pilothouses. At the end of a late 1960s navigation season on the Upper Mississippi we implemented the grand plan by sending three of our towboats downriver from St. Paul to join the ice-free, year-round navigation in Chicago. Each towboat pushed a loaded grain barge or two. Damn we felt clever. What could go wrong?

That particular year, winter arrived early and uninvited. Lake Pepin, just 50 miles downriver from St. Paul, began to make ice. Our little armada of boats and barges mule trained through the forbidding ice slabs of Pepin, the largest towboat and barge out front and the smallest, the mv. *Mendota,* taking up the rear. Despite the ice breaking ahead of it, the *Mendota* found it tough going. Capt. Don Wright radioed that it was like driving a boat through a continuous field of boulders. No one slept, partly a result of the continuous noise and partly out of fear.

Our flat-bottom boat hulls with a scow bow (absent any sort of prow) were not designed for ice breaking. Nor were the barge hulls. The *Mendota* and companions made it through Pepin, but the grain hopper barge, one with some age, began leaking dangerously. After another 80 miles of demolition derby sailing, Capt. Don put into La Crosse and left his barge load of soybeans there for the winter, with pumps running. In the warmer climes of southern Wisconsin near the Illinois-Iowa line the TCB fleet finally found flowing water and completed their trek to Chicago.

The ADM Company was not pleased with our decision to park their barge in La Crosse for the winter. But as I explained, it was either a delayed trip to the Gulf or a sunken barge and 1,400 tons of fish feed at the bottom of the Mississippi.

(l. to r.) Paul Lambert, Jack Lambert and Bob Maher aboard the new mv. St. Paul. *(1953)*

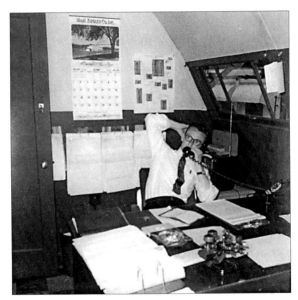

*Jack Lambert in the Quonset hut office barge.
(1950s)*

The mv. Tom Thumb *up bound on the Minnesota River, Capt. John Biles commanding. (1954)*

Jack Lambert maneuvers the launch Missfit *on a barge inspection. (1950s)*

The mv. Ohio, one of the Valley Line's converted steamers, arrives in St. Paul. (1950s)

The mv. Ruth Brent *pulls into the TCB landing for supplies. (1950s)*

TCB acquires a wharf barge to moor at its landing near the St. Paul downtown airport. (1962)

A U.S. Coast Guard cutter assists with the annual ice breaking chore on the Mississippi. (1960s)

*Towboats batter their way through winter ice on Lake Pepin.
(spring, early 1960s)*

The great flood of 1965, the record so far, covered the St. Paul downtown airport, leaving TCBs wharf barge along with some towboats and a few barges stranded.

A downriver flood leaves a gaggle of line haul towboats stranded at Lambert's Landing, in St. Paul. (1960s)

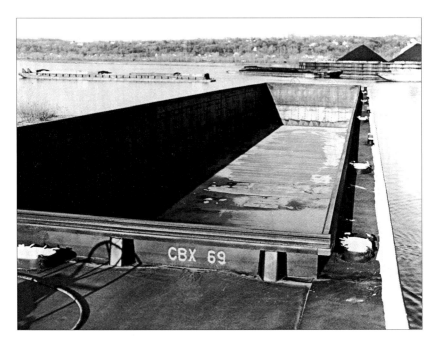

These 195-by-35-foot hopper barges are just dumb steel bathtubs, though some environmental fanatics saw them as a threat to the river environment.

TCB 301 was one of several double-skin liquid tank barges. This one was in the service of Amoco (later BP) for hauling petrochemical products. (1973)

New harbor towboats like the mv.Viking were bu
to operate under the low bridges of Chicago and
the Twin Cities. (1973)

Dredge spoil from the perimeter of St. Paul's Pigs Eye Lake was used by the Port Authority to build industrial land inside the lake. The dredged area became slips for barge fleeting. (late 1960s)

When NSP (now Xcel) built a new power plant on the Lower St. Croix River, coal barges were shuttled there from the Mississippi by TCB's mv. Sioux. (1960s)

One of TCBs retractable-pilothouse towboats pushes a pair of loads and 13 empty barges up the Minnesota River to the terminals near Savage, Minn. (1970s)

The inherent efficiency of the inland waterways is seen in this view of a 15-barge tow southbound out of St. Paul. The tow moves over 20,000 tons toward Gulf ports. More barges will be added downriver.

Barge and towboat backups like this were common in the late 1970s as river traffic confronted the failing, 41-year-old Lock and Dam 26, just above St. Louis. Railroad and environmental groups pooled lobbying efforts to prevent its replacement.

The 4,200 hp Col. George Lambert *became the queen of TCB's fleet of towboats in 1975.*

Jack and Dolly Lambert at the Chicago christening of the mv. Donald O'Toole in the mid-1970s.

Pigs Eye Lake provided a new operating base for TCB and Twin City Shipyard in the 1970s.

Part of an order for new hopper barges built by Twin City Shipyard for Canal Barge Co., of New Orleans, is moored in Pigs Eye Lake awaiting movement. TCS built a barge a week at its peak.

Packer River Terminal in late 1970s. Environmental interests fought the creation of a 1,000-foot cut to reach this existing and abandoned terminal facility near the Mississippi in South St. Paul.

Jack Lambert on the Red Sea in Saudi Arabia about 1980.

Dick Lambert, longtime TCB executive, later headed the Minnesota Dept. of Transportation Ports and Waterways office.

CHAPTER 6
Growing Pains

Expansion in both Chicago and St. Paul required additional towboats as well as a few tank barges for short-haul petroleum movements. Various nephews sought employment. One of them, Bob Bellinger, went to the River Academy and became a pilot. Doug White, my nephew-in-law, fresh from the Vietnam War, also eventually came on board. Some started as deckhands and worked their way into the office.

My eldest took over janitorial duties while still in high school. He was known as "Dan the Trash Barrel Man." Unbeknownst to me at the time, Capt. Don Wright snuck him onto a towboat for a little apprentice work at the "sticks." Scott followed in later years and worked as a deckhand on the switch boat at the St. Croix power plant. He came home each day several shades darker from coal dust. Paula neither janitored nor decked, but during her pre-journalism years in high school she took over as editor of a four-page company newsletter. Thus, like so many other river firms, we became a true family business.

The steady growth soon had us stretching our lines of credit at banks, and in 1969 we were obliged to make a public offering of our stock for further financing. It was an intriguing route to growth capital markets, and those growth capital markets would eventually help sink the barge industry. Our stock opened at $7.00 per share and did well, but I soon learned one of the hard economic lessons of life. Your mother may be proud of your past achievements, but the public investors don't give a rat's ass about the past. What matters to them is next quarter. And the hunt for more profit is a relentless master.

As if we didn't have enough problems, the St. Paul city fathers decided that all this coming and going on the river needed some supervision. The St. Paul police were directed to patrol the river, and they selected a patrolman who was near retirement and had an attitude problem. The River Cop, as we shall call him, had recently pulled his service revolver in his own home on a power-company meter reader and called for backup. The chief of police undoubtedly thought that he had put the old grouch harmlessly out to pasture.

Giving him an outboard motorboat and the freedom of the Mississippi had, however, given the River Cop a whole new set of crimes and miscreants in need of his attention. He soon graduated from delivering stern, finger-wagging lectures to recreational boaters to yelling at towboat captains about alleged speeding through the downtown portions of the river. We explained to the police department about the relative inability of a tow to speed and the need to maintain headway for steerage. Apparently the message did not get passed on to the River Cop.

He chased the mv. *Harry Harris* pushing a loaded barge downstream through the St. Paul bridges, demanding that Capt. Harry, "pull over." It was a case of the irascible meeting the intractable. Once Harris had landed his barge, the River Cop tied up alongside the towboat, read him the riot act and gave him a ticket for speeding. Capt. Harry was not cowed and chose to challenge the matter in court, and we attended the session to support him.

The speeding ticket went away. But before the River Cop would get his well-deserved retirement, he turned a routine Sunday outing into a major criminal event. The cop spotted a small houseboat proceeding upriver at what seemed to him an unreasonable speed. A long chase ensued, the boater unaware of the police outboard trailing behind and trying to catch up. Unable to close the gap between the boats, River Cop fired a warning round, apparently soundless to the boater over the roar of his own engine. Enraged by this apparent disdain for police authority, River Cop then put a shot through the back wall of the houseboat. Fortunately for the three family members aboard (mother, father and small child), no one was hit.

The St. Paul Police quickly turned over their river patrol duties to the county sheriff, and a grateful TCB provided a small steel launch.

◈ ◈ ◈

TCB continued its inevitable periodic encounters with the extreme current caused by flood runoff. One of the most memorable and potentially deadly occurred on the Minnesota River under strange circumstances. A new highway bridge had been built a few miles below Port Cargill to replace the old Cedar Avenue swing bridge. Before the old bridge (close to the Black Dog Power Plant) could be removed, we engaged it in battle and lost.

The old steel bridge sat on a center pier in the middle of the river, and was opened by a tender to a position parallel with the channel, after road traffic had been stopped. Our towboat mv. *Santee*, down bound with loaded grain barges, blew for the bridge. The bridge tender dutifully swung the center section to the parallel position one last time, but for some reason the old mass of steel hit the stops and then bounced back a few feet. The *Santee*'s barges were already sliding through the opening. Our pilot (name lost to antiquity) blew his whistle again and again and began furiously backing his twin diesels, but the current was such that he could not kill his headway, and while the loaded barges slid blissfully through the opening, the lower steel framework of the swing span loomed closer, like a bulldozer blade pointed at the *Santee* pilothouse. Slowly, inexorably, despite the bleating of the air horn, the *Santee* met the steel girders of the bridge. It was not a contest between equals.

The bridge crushed the upper portion of the pilothouse like it was a matchbox, managing to kill the headway. The crew found our pilot unhurt on the floor, under the girders but crying like your kid sister, perhaps understandably. The encounter hastened the removal of the old Cedar Avenue structure as well as the retirement of the pilot from his chosen profession.

Well we had attacked a few bridges. Perhaps it was just our turn to lose.

CHAPTER 7

ENVIRONMENTAL WARS

In the late 1960s the St. Paul Port Authority began an industrialization plan that called for dredging the area abounding Pigs Eye Lake (on the far southeast corner of the city limits). The backwater dredging created barge slips on the Mississippi side of Pigs Eye, and the fill was used to build up the inside bank of the lake for the waterfront industry. Needless to say, it was raised to a level above the 100-year flood line. Twin City Barge took a lease on the barge parking areas on the channel as well as the some of the newly "manufactured" land inside the lake. On the latter we built a new shipyard facility and an office. We imported John Buursema, a first class naval architect from Holland via Morgan City, La., to get us into the barge building business.

This innovative project by the St. Paul Port Authority eased in under the radar of the environmental movement, then in its infancy.

Local "save Mother Earth" advocates were mostly middle aged and female, an intense and humorless lot. Having raised their children, the fanatic ones were now prepared to turn their energy on bigger and weightier matters: power plants, heavy industry and the barge business. At neighborhood councils they laid plans to proscribe appropriate simplistic uses of the national waterway. Lacking experience or knowledge, they seemed to have the notion that all business should be conducted in tall glass buildings where papers were shuffled. Never mind the production of petroleum or electric energy, manufacture of goods, or feeding the world with our agricultural bounty. Those were just bothersome details not within the purview of those out to save the heron and carp of Pigs Eye Lake.

They began to show up at Port Authority meetings (their right) as "interested citizens" to protest virtually everything on the agenda. They even complained about the "visual" pollution of our new fabricating shop, the color of corrugated sheet metal buildings throughout the world, and our yard cranes, painted yellow for safety reasons. The local business baiters wanted earth tones. With more than a little sarcasm, I asked if they would want the fab shop repainted white with the coming of each winter.

I argued with the extremists on many occasions but soon learned that fanatics, of whatever ilk, are endowed with such religious fervor that they care not for facts or consequences, and the Commerce Clause and balance of trade be damned.

After clashing with them repeatedly, I tried to make nice. We took dozens of them on board towboats to cruise the local rivers, showing them that we were not spewing pollutants and doing nothing to cause hysteria within the heron rookery. In fact, as the activists lined the rail, we passed close by a rank of herons standing on a barge looking back, each group observing the other with grouchy stares. To counter their perceptions of towboats, we pointed out our lack of a bow wave compared to that of the small-engined runabouts. And we showed them that the cargo-carrying barges themselves were just dumb steel tubs with no discharge to the river. Seeing the continuous discharge of engine cooling water from the towboat, one of the ladies assumed an, "Ah-ha" sort of attitude, and seemed disappointed to hear that it was not waste discharging from our bilge or toilets — all of which went into shore-side disposal and thence to treatment — but rather circulating river water.

On the cusp of converting to low-sulphur, western coal, regional power companies proposed a rail-to-water transfer terminal in Pigs Eye Lake, and the Port Authority drew up plans to accommodate the new cargo-transfer operation. The north end of Pigs Eye Lake was bordered by several railroads. The concept was logistically sound. All of the power plants were already situated on the river to receive barged coal from southern Illinois and western Kentucky. Unit trains of the western coal could simply be reloaded to barges for delivery to the existing river terminals.

This was too much for the environmentalists, who consolidated into a tribe called the Pigs Eye Coalition. Their goals were those of urban industrial anarchists. They had badgered the public utilities about their use of high-sulphur coal, but damned if they would permit the infusion of the newly acceptable coal into the electric system with facilities already in place. They won the argument at the level of the St. Paul City Council, which vetoed the Pigs Eye coal-transfer facility. Thus each of the area power plants, including some in Wisconsin, were obliged to build a rail loop for the receipt of 100-car unit trains. The electric utilities passed on the cost of the several new rail transfer operations to the unwary consumers.

One of the most rabid and active of the environmental advocates showed up at an annual shareholders meeting of TCB. Her husband, a man with a perverse sense of humor, had purchased a small amount of TCB stock so that she could be privy to the nefarious deeds of us polluting capitalists. Finding herself surrounded by happy stockholders, she couldn't quite figure out a strategy to derail us, so she contented herself with taking voluminous notes and sending loathing glares at one and all.

However, as the Sierra Club and Isaac Walton League joined these local movements, the extremists prevailed throughout the United States. They had endless axes to be ground, and politicians counted their numbers. It was the nadir of industrial progress. We weren't outlawed or removed by eminent domain, but the 1980s saw the gradual decline of heavy industry with the rise of the National Environmental Policy Act (NEPA) and its unintended handmaiden, globalization. Whatever the need or rationale, NEPA served as a device for those afflicted with the need to rebel against heavy industry. Now in the 21st century we wail about the need for good manufacturing jobs and the mystery that many of those jobs seem to have magically evaporated.

❖❖❖

The lash of the investment bankers was continuous and unrelenting — more profits. Diversification was then in vogue, so we sought other areas of expansion that seemed allied to what we did. When a liquid barge terminal in South Chicago's Lake Calumet hung out the "For Sale" sign, our investment experts thought it was a promising fit. It was along our waterway avenue in the Chicago area and offered a haven for our boats and fleeting for our barges. What I knew about chemical storage wouldn't fill a thimble, but a competent staff went with Bulk Terminals, then a subsidiary of Union Tank Car Corp. The price was modest because UTLX, as it was known in the rail business, was divesting. That should have set off the alarms for us, but by the mid-70s it seemed that we could do no wrong. Only a few months after the acquisition, a pressure valve on a tank of exotic chemicals sprung a leak and released chemicals into the air as a fine yellow mist that sent an irritating fog over a high-rise, low-income housing development. The resulting lawsuits were a bonanza for the local trial attorneys and a disaster for our stock. We quickly unloaded the terminal to a foreign shipping company.

However, we had already begun the creation of a dry bulk barge terminal in South St. Paul, across the river from the shipyard. The site of this effort was an abandoned piece of property owned by Boise Cascade Corp. The vacant land held a huge bulk warehouse, an enormous truck pad, easy access to highways and was alongside a rail connection. All it lacked was a direct connection with the river (also Boise land) just some 600 feet away. Returning this property to a useful state involved dredging an access channel, installing a truck dump grain leg and, not incidentally, the creation of jobs and more property taxes for the city and county. We named it Packer River Terminal. What could be wrong with this plan?

The environmental interests fought us again. Even a member of the South St. Paul City Council found a nearby resident who said the noise of the terminal would lower her property values. We noted that her existing neighbors, to our immediate south and west, were a gun club and the main line of the Omaha Railroad.

By this time the St. Paul District Corps of Engineers had acquired an environmental expert (courtesy of NEPA), and in order to justify his existence he suggested that we needed an environmental impact statement to dig the barge cut through our own property. The colonel in charge took the easy route and agreed that we needed the tedious impact statement, although there were no virgin forests to be cut down or snail darters to be displaced. Not even his associates in the Corps in Washington agreed, but it was impolitic at that point in time to fight against the environmental tide. So we waded through the process as if we had proposed digging a barge channel through to Yellowstone Park. We got the permit but it took several months and started my growth of gray hair.

CHAPTER 8
THE RIVER CONVENTIONS

In the dead of the God-awful Midwest winter doldrums the river industry held a yearly convention, actually a party, usually in St. Louis, now and then in Chicago. This gathering was sponsored by a national waterway association and occurred, ostensibly, to promote waterway development, with much harumphing about the Northwest Ordinance of 1787, etc. River carriers and shippers spent more time discussing business and even more time partying. Wherever the convention was held, there were hospitality suites that witnessed prodigious imbibing. Although booze was forbidden on river towboats, river men in general were not inclined toward temperance.

There was an initial exchange on arrival at the convention that was akin to a lodge ritual. The folks from St. Louis greeted the northerners with, "Is it cold enough for you?"

We responded, "This is nothing. Back in the Twin Cities it's much colder than this."

"Oh but here in St. Louis it's a moist cold, much worse than your dry cold."

Just try to convince a northerner that there is something worse than 30 degrees below zero. Then we all retired to the nearest watering hole for some antifreeze. The favorite was the Temple of Culture, run by St. Louis Ship and its subsidiary Federal Barge Line. It seemed to be open at any hour of the day or night. And they poured spirits for customers and competitors alike, as did all of the hospitality rooms. We river rats were a fraternity regardless of corporate affiliation. Herman Pott held forth at the Temple as burgomaster, and Art Parsons, along with Pete Fanchi, headed the welcoming committee. When sufficiently lubricated, Art led the singing.

There were daytime meetings of this and that committee to pass resolutions on various matters that would be taken very seriously by our congressmen and then largely ignored. The navigable waterways had had their day in the sun. They had been developed, and little in the way of new projects came forth as a result of heavy lobbying, save the Arkansas Waterway and the Tenn-Tom canal. It was the twilight of channel development in the Heartland, but still senators McClellan, Russell, Stennis and others showed up to speak at the banquet to ensure us that they were behind the promotion of this or that civil-works project. As for the businessmen present, our eyes tended to glaze over at these political fulminations about new projects yet to be realized, and we said, mostly to each other, that it would be great if the government could just maintain the channels we had.

The Upper Mississippi Waterway Association (UMWA), of which I was a member and sometime chairman, had its own pet projects, like the Minnesota River and a pair of locks in the Minneapolis Upper Harbor. The former was a cheap fix for a stretch of water that eventually carried a river of grain to export markets. The latter was a gleam in the eye of Minneapolis politicians like Mayor and later Senator Hubert Humphrey, and was ultimately completed despite dubious cost-benefit ratios.

The UMWA had its own hospitality suite at the national conventions in order to win friends and, ostensibly, influence people. Pols and union leaders from both Minneapolis and St. Paul rallied at the suite to show their support and partake of our refreshments.

One year a delegation from the city of Minneapolis appeared (doubtless at taxpayers expense) to lend their authority to the deliberations. One city official, a man always full of himself, appeared with the wife. Gene Kirchoff (CEO at Packer River Terminal) asked the charming, matronly grandmother if she would like something to drink. She allowed as how she was rather thirsty and asked what we had. Gene ran down the list of possible soft drinks, wine and then hard liquor, hesitating as Mrs. X continued to look thoughtful. Then he reeled off the names of a few exotic cocktails that the hired bartender could create. Finally she said, "I think I'll have one of those martini drinks."

The martini was concocted, and Mrs. X chug-a-lugged it. Seeing her glass suddenly empty, Gene inquired as to whether or not he could get her anything else.

"Thank you young man. That was very good, I think I'll have another."

"It's hard to caution someone old enough to be your mother," Gene said later. And besides, Councilman X was right there, although in deep discussion about the Upper and Lower St. Anthony Lock project. So Gene served the dear lady a second martini, which also vanished in about two swallows. Seeming as sober as a preacher, she waved the empty glass in the air toward Gene, now her personal waiter. As river talk, of which she took no notice, swirled about her a third martini was placed in her hand. This she sipped, while Gene and I began an unobtrusive surveillance.

Would she like a chair, we inquired.

"No thank you," but she did get one shoulder up against a wall, and her smiling demeanor began a slow transformation. Her facial expression changed from happy to questioning: "Who the hell are all these people, and what am I doing here?" Then she cocked her hat over one eye and began an almost imperceptible (except to Gene and me) rocking on her pumps.

We inquired more loudly of the lady, so that the husband would hear us, about a chair.

She said, "No!" rather emphatically, implying, "Bugger off!"

Mr. X got to her side just as she began to sag down the wall. He tried to get hold under her arms, but they flopped straight up in the air as she began her rag doll impersonation. Her husband, a large man, departed with her in his grip, although she was doing little to assist the exit. We felt awful and determined to be more circumspect in offering the more exotic drinks. Fortunately, the councilman was much too important a person to know who we were.

Convention recollections are legion, but I still recall with amusement the evening when the last people had departed the UMWA suite and I was cleaning up with Bill Frenzel, later a great congressman from Minnesota. We heard a faint noise in the rather large coat closet near the entrance of the suite and saw a light under the door. Opening carefully we discovered one of our members, Bob Miller, standing quietly, his eyes shut, humming. We woke him as gently as possible and he looked startled. "Oh my God! I thought I was in the elevator!"

I do not wish to imply that we were the only ones to partake of the golden nectar during the convention. One evening I was escorting Joe Shiely, St. Paul's aggregate king, on his first convention. We were between hospitality rooms when we encountered one of the gang of good old boys from Greenville, Miss., in the hallway. He greeted me with, "Hey, shakhowyawl."

Joe asked if that was authentic Cajun talk, so I had to translate and explain that it was just authentic whiskey talk.

For many years we took the train to the convention site, when trains were still an option. Then Braniff or Northwest Air Lines became more certain modes. Passenger rail travel was rushing toward its own demise, and we might have been in on its death knell. After taking an overnight train from the Twin Cities to St. Louis in the mid 1960s, we boarded the return leg of the Rock Island Rocket back home. As we slept, the northbound line was engulfed by a major winter storm blowing through Iowa. Each of us awakened early in the dark and freezing cold, the heat having gone off. We stumbled out of our compartments to complain to any rail employee we could collar and were met with the news of the blizzard and advised that the ice-laden locomotive was just then struggling, like the "Little Engine that Could," into Cedar Rapids, Iowa, not St. Paul.

The passenger cars were left on a siding while the diesel locomotive chugged a couple of tracks away. It was to be placed in a nearby round house for thawing. As we shivered and pondered our fate, we could see two railroad employees chipping ice off the locomotive with ball-peen hammers. The scene could not have been more incongruous had they had been assaulting a dinosaur with croquet mallets. One of the workers threw his hammer at ice near the roof of the engine cab and it came hurtling back almost braining his partner. It had become the Laurel and Hardy Line.

The situation became hilarious, but it was also readily obvious that this passenger line was doomed. When passengers discovered that the diner had no food and the bar car had been left farther back to lighten the load, the mood grew ugly. But there was nowhere to go. We weren't even near the Cedar Rapids station. Fortunately, we far-sighted river men had retained some of the convention-suite stock that had escaped consumption. So we survived, but it was a near thing. The overnight Rocket finally chugged into St. Paul at 6 p.m., 24 hours after its departure from St. Louis. We never took the train again.

A year later Tom Talbert, an Upper Mississippi coal baron, arranged for the charter of a Braniff flight to and from St. Louis. Christy Murnane, another of the coal guys, took over the galley and tried to serve the passengers with "Moose Milk," a concoction of whiskey and regular milk. The drink dishonored both ingredients.

◈◈◈

Some of the river brethren's unique gatherings included an extraordinary Brit who was the Lloyds of London representative to U.S. waterway interests. Bryan Wakeham was a highly educated product of England, a former Guards officer and a marine insurance expert. He must have found us an odd lot but visited the Colony frequently and was a wonderful host on the rare occasions when any of us were in London.

I passed through London twice during my years in the barge-line business and once got the grand tour of Lloyds, courtesy of Bryan. It was an extraordinary place, feeling something like the New York stock exchange but more gentlemanly. No shouting, no voices being raised. The various insurance syndicates were each in little cubicles filled with ring binders full of papers describing the insured property and the various groups that had bought into that property for insurance coverage. This was in the days before computers, and most everything was done with typed or hand-written notes that were inserted in the coverage binders. Lloyds would provide the excess coverage for the potential catastrophe over and above basic insurance. We called the coverage an "umbrella," the folks at Lloyds termed it a "bumbershoot." As such, they insured everything from barges and towboats to the anatomy of Hollywood stars, i.e. Betty Grable's legs.

The only indication of any automation within this vast and ancient insurance undertaking was the clacking of teletypes that would announce a sinking in the Straits of Magellan or a pirate attack on a vessel in the Straits of Malacca. But there was no shouting, just a few muttered comments like, "Oh I say, bad show." On occasion the U.S. river industry would show up with a fleet breakaway or some flood-related sinkings. Lord knows we needed such coverage.

On one of his visits with his American river clients, Bryan joined us at a meeting in Marco Island, Fla. After a hard day of whatever it was that we did, several of our wives met us for a nightcap at a bar in a posh hotel. A small, unappreciated orchestra played in one end of the room, while we occupied a large table and told each other funny river stories. We were not being boisterous by our standards, but the management said that the musicians had complained that we were drowning them out. When one of our group noted that this wasn't exactly Carnegie Damn Hall, we were asked to leave.

Bryan Wakeham, sober as a vicar, looked stunned and said thoughtfully, "My word, I don't think I've ever been ejected from a public house."

We all howled. That's what he got for hanging around with river rats.

Chapter 9
Lambert of Arabia

During my first 20 years in the barge business I had come in contact with a number of people associated with petrochemicals, as we had begun to move liquid products. TCB had an asphalt tow under contract to AMOCO, barging hot asphalt throughout the midriver region. One of the oil people suggested that there was a similar need for modern barge transportation in the Red Sea, and he had contacts in Saudi Arabia he wanted me to meet.

It was the mid-70s, and since TCB was doing well, profits appeared stable, and a consulting fee was being offered, the investigation seemed to have little risk. Our Saudi contact was the president of an oil refinery in Jeddah, Dr. Abdulhadi Taher. He was American-educated and spoke English better than most Americans. We had an initial meeting in London followed by subsequent trips to Jeddah. All of this led to nothing. Even the consulting fees dried up before all the invoices had been tendered. However, visits to the ancient Arab kingdom were unforgettable for a kid from the Midwest.

God had forgotten the Arabian Peninsula when it came to water but blessed it with oil. For the most part the country looked like Arizona: deserts and hard-scrabble hills just 20 degrees north of the equator. Its vast oil deposits lay mostly in the east near the Persian Gulf. A pipeline had been built across the peninsula to Jeddah, on the Red Sea. There were few roads in Saudi Arabia, and all of the existing ones fanned out from the sole refinery at Jeddah, which produced asphalt and other petroleum products.

Taher was considering whether or not he could expedite road building by transporting asphalt and various refined products in Red Sea tank barges, rather than in small truckload lots. After London, where Taher outlined his ideas, we flew to Jeddah twice to further our research. There being no rivers in Saudi Arabia (Only depressions, known as "wadis," hinted at ancient water courses.) it was not irrational to consider use of the Red Sea as another transportation route. However, the long slender Red Sea (barely 200 miles across at its widest) was full of shoal water, ending with the Farason Banks near the southern border with Yemen. The narrow, deep-draft shipping lanes from the Gulf of Aden north to Suez were well marked. However, there seemed to be no good topographic maps of the rest of the sea, and the only coastal activity was by shallow-draft Arab dhows, unsuited for liquids.

The government agencies of Saudi Arabia were small fiefdoms, and dropping Taher's name did not elicit cooperation from port authorities or commerce officials. Although the U.S. Army Corps of Engineers had a large Mideast Division in the capitol, Riyadh, they were concentrating on infrastructure and not waterway transportation.

In the 1970s Saudi Arabia had tons of money and little else. Water and sewage systems and cities with high-rise buildings were being constructed. We were shown a brand new, state-of-the-art hospital in Jeddah that had more doctors and nurses than patients.

If you fell off your camel and broke your leg, it was apparently considered unmanly to go to the hospital. The tribal healer handled that sort of thing while the victim bit on a bullet.

Jeddah was a relatively modern city. Alongside the modern shopping centers were traditional Arab markets, the "souks," where haggling was an art form. In both the souks and the newer parts of Jeddah we saw women covered from head to foot (the abayah) with only their eyes showing and lots of morals police who eyed strangers warily. Having just come from England and the States, where hot pants and tank tops were coming into vogue, it was astonishingly medieval. The few women we did see in the workplace were foreign imports from other Arab nations. Virtually all of the workingmen were foreign. The Saudis were mostly entrepreneurs or warriors.

Women did not drive. And men did so without any 10-2 nonsense on the steering wheel. One hand was sufficient for steering (usually at break-neck speed) while the other was used to bear down on the horn.

Taher's son, a suave, educated, well-spoken young man, took us to dinner at a restaurant atop the tallest building in Jeddah. Over an excellent meal, we watched a glorious sunset beyond the Red Sea. But there was no before, during or after alcohol. Nor were there spirits in any hotels. We had been warned that alcohol was strictly forbidden throughout the kingdom. That's why we never held a river convention there. The Arabs were officially afflicted with sobriety. The story was told among Westerners that a large crate marked "piano" had been delivered at the Port of Jeddah for the British Embassy. As it hit the dock a tinkle was heard and some mysterious liquid oozed from the planks. The police summoned a member of the embassy staff to explain. "Not ours," insisted the proper Englishman. "The crate must have been mislabeled. The British Embassy wouldn't have a piano that leaked."

Most of the time we were on our own for hotel meals in a town that was dry, nor were we invited to a Taher home. Home entertainment was apparently not practiced by the upper class. However, for some obtuse reason we did get invited to the home of an Arab construction magnate along with several other westerners. The host, whose name I cannot recall, (bin Host) was the son of a tribal leader. The tribal sheik disdained matters of business and finance in favor of his tent and herds, but was honored by the royal family with a construction franchise. Hence, a son had been sent to the big city to conduct business (a token CEO), while Americans or Brits actually ran things.

Bin Host's single-story compound was of Arizona style construction but seemed to ramble off out of sight behind vast walls. We never saw his wife or any children. The meal, a prodigious one as it proved, was prepared by male servants in a kitchen that did not lack for a single appliance. The American manager of the construction firm and his wife were present, along with a British gent and his two young daughters, the women all modestly dressed but still in glaring contrast to what we saw on the streets. Before dinner a serving cart was rolled in with a bottle of every known liquor. We gratefully tipped a few while bin Host entertained us with music from his complex tape system, a series of reels and amplifiers that covered one wall. He apparently had only one Western tape, the St. Louis Blues March, played over and over at a crushing decibel level.

When summoned to the dining area, we beheld a beautiful tablecloth with many fruits and a huge platter containing the main course — an entire lamb, head and all — sitting amidst a small ocean of rice turned green by limes. But there was no table. We were invited to squat on small pillows where the chairs would have been. The chef stepped between a pair of the guests onto the tablecloth and began to carve pieces of the lamb. We each had a modest serving, declining the eyeballs and adjacent portions of the head.

Our gracious host spoke little English, but then I spoke not a word of Arabic. However, with a great flourish and much smiling, he offered me a vegetable that looked like a small green pepper. The American business manager translated: "Eating this will make you good with the ladies tonight."

What ladies? I had none with me and I couldn't imagine I was supposed to jump the American wife or the British girls after dessert. However, not wanting to be a party pooper, I nibbled at the green finger.

"No, no!" exhorted bin Host. I was to take the whole thing in one bite.

Since I had lubricated myself with a bit of scotch, and had managed to avoid either bow or stern of the lamb, I decided to be a sport. How much harm could a little green pepper do? Swallowing was like a swig of Napalm. I seized my water glass (no wine at dinner) and downed its contents. Then I chugged the water tumbler of the American lady next to me.

Our host laughed like a chimp, while I felt as if smoke might be coming from my ears.

◇ ◇ ◇

Having accomplished virtually nothing of consequence, I returned to the States. The flight from Jeddah to Riyadh was on Saudia Air Lines. One of the passengers was an old tribal sheik with flowing robes and a ceremonial dagger at his waist. Behind him were three retainers, also in Arab headdress and robes. One held the sheik's hooded falcon and the other two were guards, complete with bandoliers of ammunition and rifles. These hawk-nosed, mustachioed, dears all glared at Westerners like we might be candidates for summary execution.

At Riyadh we transferred to Olympic Airways (Greek) and were offered champagne as soon as the door closed. We were back in civilization. A few Arab men and women had also boarded, but none had rifles or large carnivorous birds. Once out of Saudi air space a few of the abayah-covered ladies went to the lavatory and emerged without head scarves or robes, in very stylish western haute couture fashions.

Thus ended my attempt at imposing barges and tugboats on the Red Sea. Conceptually the idea was sound, but like Moses I couldn't get the natives to cooperate.

CHAPTER 10

THE PERILS OF WASHINGTON, D.C.

For a century or more water transport moved cargo within the United States, where the rivers provided the first natural highways of commerce. Modest improvements fostered that growth, benefitting the contiguous regions.

With the drive west in the mid-1800s, railroading exploded. The rail expansion was encouraged by a federal government that lavished aid on it in the form of land grants and exclusive routes. At the turn of the century Washington discovered, to its amazement, that those railroads were not treating the nation with motherly love, as they had hoped. So Congress decided to fix the problem by enacting anti-trust legislation and forming the regulatory Interstate Commerce Commission (ICC).

Washington also began the slow process of rebuilding the river transportation system with the slack-water locks and dams we know today, bringing the controlled channel depth to nine feet. That effort provided thousands of jobs for a depression-ridden country as we poured enough concrete to pave the Sahara. The federal government even operated the first modern barge line, the Inland Waterways Corporation, later known as Federal Barge Line.

The growth of the Upper Mississippi River system was largely completed about the time of World War II. One of its unexpected benefits was that small-ship construction could be undertaken at inland yards, even at the far northern end of navigation. Sub chasers were built at St. Paul's Dingle Boat Works, and landing craft were built at Savage on the Minnesota River. The growth of barge transportation on the new tributaries was largely deferred until after the war but then expanded steadily, because the post-war economy was surging and communities welcomed the benefits of bulk transportation for public power and agriculture.

However, after the interstate highway program had gotten a running start in the post-World War II era, Washington decided that things were going too well, and again it was time for congressional tinkering. The railroads had ramped up their incessant lobbying for some help against both highway and waterway traffic. Because of the sneering indifference of the Department of Transportation to waterways, we had dubbed it the "Department of Trains."

The railroads were basically frustrated with the transportation marketplace as it reacted to competition. The free market was at work, but in its unique way of fixing something that wasn't broken Washington embarked on a whole range of drastic legislation — the kind with unintended consequences.

The 1970s saw several pieces of legislation (the 3R Act, the 4R Act) to relieve the railroads of the obligations that had been attached to their franchises. And government, hell bent on deregulation, began to dismantle the spider-web-like Interstate Commerce Act. In less than a decade Congress tossed 100 years of transportation legislation in the trash bin of history.

About this time, a delegation of us went to whine at Senator Russell Long, of Louisiana, a longtime waterway advocate. "Yawl better get used to it boys. In a few more years this deregulation will leave us with just six air lines, six railroads and six barge lines."

We left his office thinking that the old man was losing his marbles, but he was just short of being a prophet.

Our barge-line brethren in the South seemed certain that their congressional supporters would not let us down. But the railroads and environmentalists outnumbered us. We had no giant unions to support us, because we were too labor efficient. And we had no public support, because who ever shipped anything by barge? We were unknown to the general public.

Even the succor of deregulation was not enough for the railroads. They pushed for punitive measures against the barge industry: user fees and limits on system maintenance.

A vital lock just below the Upper Mississippi-Illinois River confluence, Lock 26, at Alton, Ill., built between 1934 and 38, had become the waterway's Achilles heel. The 360-foot auxiliary chamber was the smallest in the system, forcing tows to be broken into several sections before transiting up or down. In addition the structure was failing. Erosion under the river wall of the lock chamber was apparent. Dye infused in the chamber leaked under the reinforced concrete monolith to the river. The adjoining dam was also being subjected to serious scouring. These structural deficiencies caused the Corps of Engineers to predict that disaster was possible. Navigation could be imperiled.

I joined the lobbying frenzy in D.C., prompted by Braxton Beauregard Culpepper Carr, head of the barge industries' trade association, American Waterway Operators (AWO). Along with many others from the barge business, we began visiting the Capitol to inform our congressional delegations of the problem and the critical nature of barge operations to electric utilities and the export-grain trade.

We formed a Lock and Dam 26 Committee, headed by a former Minnesota congressional staff member. He managed to get us an audience at the Carter White House, albeit with some low level, self-important staff twerp. The highlight of that meeting took place during the security check. Some uniformed Secret Service palace guard, who looked like he bench-pressed twerps, met us just inside the West Wing doors and, scanning a list of our names and affiliations, said, "Where's Jack Lambert?"

I pushed through, warily offering my Minnesota drivers license. He ignored the license and said, with his impostor glare, "You're not Jack Lambert." He had been expecting the Pittsburgh Steelers linebacker, like himself a man of some serious dimension.

Those seeking to prevent the replacement of Lock 26 formed a counter alliance, alleging that they only had the nation's best fiscal interests at heart. The railroads' strange new bedfellows included the Sierra Club, the Isaac Walton League and assorted tree huggers. The "Knock the Lock" gang even put out a periodical newspaper attempting to inform and rally public opinion. It was filled with misinformation and blather about how the river was in general being ruined by the Corps of Engineers and the barge lines, and should be returned to its pristine state where Hiawatha had once paddled his canoe.

Something about the address of that journal prompted me to look up their office in the Windy City. It turned out to be on an upper floor of the Chicago Northwestern Railroad. I was suitably enraged but tickled with my investigative effort.

The case for the immediate replacement of old Lock and Dam 26 was by no means an easy one. The possibility of a disaster made our corporate blood run cold but seemed unlikely to Washington.

In great detail, we explained that if a disaster stopped river shipping, there wouldn't be enough alternative transportation capacity to pick up the slack. Barge lines moved export grain in 1,400-ton lots and the rails in 100-ton hopper cars. Even with 100-car unit trains, the rail gateways in The Gulf and on the West Coast had serious limitations. The vast unit-train rail loops imposed constrictions on volume. They could only handle a fraction of the waterway load. And we were the most energy-efficient mode.

You could see Congress members' interest begin to flag as they tried to distill our facts. As with other issues, government seemed incapable of putting economic problems into perspective. Bill Frenzel, who had been in the House of Representatives for a term or two, tried to help us understand: "Congress only acts quickly in Pearl Harbor-type scenarios."

And then in the midst of the rail-barge battle, President Jimmy Carter imposed a Russian grain embargo. The president sought to punish the Soviets for the invasion of Afghanistan, but his victim was the American farmer. We barge-line guys were just collateral damage. The grain embargo was unworkable (as it had been when Nixon tried it in 1973) because of the international nature of the export-grain trade, soybeans from Brazil were as good as soybeans from Minnesota. The Carter effort only lasted six months but further confused the transportation issue.

The high-profile transportation war propelled the matter of waterway user fees to the forefront. Since the earliest days of the republic, the right of passage on the waterways had been declared free to all. The champion of waterway user fees was Sen. Pete Dominici, of New Mexico, a state renowned for cattle and cactus but not waterways and export grain. Along with many others, I had appeared before him to testify. He did all the talking. It was more like an inquisition in which Dominici treated us as the personification of evil. My own senator, Wendell Anderson, sat at the committee table and, though loquacious by nature, he failed to come to my rescue or utter a thought — in a convenient coma.

Our long and diligent efforts in the trenches of Washington finally yielded the necessary approval for the replacement of ailing Lock and Dam 26. But the ransom was a barge industry user fee, a tax on diesel fuel, followed by a second tax.

◈◈◈

During one of many visits to the nation's capital, I was with Charlie Lehman and Wayne Musgrove in a limousine making the rounds. As we left a stoplight, a small yellow MG with Minnesota plates passed us. It was unmistakably my son Scott's car. At the time he was an aide to Congressman Bill Frenzel. I noted the car to my companions, and in his best Hollywood dialog Wayne ordered the driver to "Catch that car!" As we pulled alongside the MG, Wayne and Charlie leaned toward the open window, yelling and waving. I was furthest from the window, in the dark of the rear, and it took Scott a few seconds to recognize the besiegers in the mafia-like hit car before he had to turn left toward the House Office Building. His passenger, another aide, failing to recognize anyone, and bewildered by the encounter, had to be assured that his life had not been in peril. It was one of the few light moments in the D.C. lobbying battles.

Chapter 11
The Investor-Barge Virus

B y 1980 TCB had harbor operations in Chicago and the Twin Cities, a barge line with over 300 dry and liquid barges, a production shipyard, and a bulk-cargo terminal in South St. Paul. I had started with just a $5,000 investment. Now I owed various lenders about $50 million. TCB stock had risen from $7 per share to over $20. Only in America. Just about the time I considered myself the boy genius of the waterways, the roof was beginning to cave in.

The steady growth of river commerce that had cascaded over from the 50s into the 80s was about to reach its peak and start a decades-long decline. A logistical shift — a sea change — was beginning in northbound cargo. Coal from southern Illinois and western Kentucky, long a staple of the dry-cargo carriers, began giving way to low-sulphur western coal. In the Twin Cities alone, four power plants that had been fed for decades by barged southern coal began the transition to unit trainloads of Powder River Basin, western coal. Northbound dry cargo was eventually reduced largely to salt and fertilizer.

That was not the worst of it. A calamity thundered toward the barge business like a train wreck in the night. Few were aware of the impending collision, and no amount of last-minute effort could flag down the trains of financial doom: investor barges and falling freight rates. (And Al Gore hadn't yet invented corn-based ethanol to further reduce the flow of export grain.)

In the late 1970s investors had begun taking an interest in barges — not investing in barge lines but in floating equipment. A handful of St. Louis river men saw that their well-heeled friends were investing in shopping malls and vacation complexes, and looking for new ways to diversify their portfolios. Why not barges? Banks and conventional leasing companies had financed river carriers for years based on the perceived needs of the barge industry. Individual investors offered a whole new source of capital. Individuals and investor groups began to order new barges based on their unquestioned belief in barges as a tax shelter, rather than on the demands of river freight volume.

The new leasing scheme involved a few wealthy folks exposed to barge investments by their friends. For example, there was a grain hopper barge operating out of Minneapolis with the number "NVB 1." The nominal owner, who chartered this barge to a carrier, was Norm Van Brocklin, recent head coach of the Minnesota Vikings. He might have known a barge from a blocking dummy, but his knowledge of water transportation was nil. It was a classic fixed-fee charter for a few dollars above the debt service that allowed both parties to make a profit. But the investor-barge boom that hit the river in the late 1970s was a dramatic variation on the old charter theme.

Managers of these new fleets of investor barges sold shares in a partnership that owned barges. The managers booked freight, provided for towing and maintained the equipment. Most investors had no more appreciation of the barge business than coach

Van Brocklin, nor did they care. Theoretically, they would be paid from the stream of freight income, after the managers deducted the direct operating costs and a management fee. Best of all for the investor, his legitimate taxable ordinary income was sheltered by the 10 percent investment tax credit (ITC) and accelerated depreciation generated by the barge investment, then permitted by the tax codes. The ITC and depreciation were non-cash expenses, yet a legal deduction from other real income. Hence a dentist, attorney or NFL coach could shelter his or her salary with the ITC and accelerated depreciation from the barge deal.

It all worked out on paper, or so it seemed. New York investment bankers saw the play and couldn't resist getting into the game. They made it big league. Millions of dollars were solicited nationwide in prospectuses that forecast grand sheltered earnings. As has so often been proven over the years, Wall Street only knew what the snake oil salesmen were telling them. Their research analysts barely knew where the waterway system was, much less the cargo demands of river shippers. A Kidder Peabody prospectus projected an income stream from covered grain barges that would attract over 200 percent of the 1975 benchmark freight rate for each of ten annual trips from the Upper Mississippi River to the Gulf. And if things didn't work out quite as promised, the barges could be moved. Just try to move a shopping mall or a Florida golf-condo complex.

When the greatest deluge of investor barge proposals were hawked, freight rates for grain were, in fact, over 200 percent of the old 1975 tariff rate, the last published rates set by the ICC before commerce deregulation was established. And round trips on the Upper Mississippi had never exceeded seven or eight barge loads per year under average operating conditions. With spring floods and tough winter ice, the navigation season was rarely over eight months, sometimes no longer than seven. It usually took a month for a barge to make the round trip down and back with hand-offs from one tow to another and with loading and unloading delays. Ten round trips was an anomaly.

Nor were freight rates as predictable and stable as they had been when shippers and carriers negotiated rates. Barge cargo rates for bulk commodities became driven by barge supply and demand, as freight itself had become a commodity, traded at the St. Louis Merchants Exchange along with grain and pork bellies. This late development had been fostered by the grain business. And the few rate quotes posted each day became the basis from which all barge grain transport began to be priced. Freight rates thus established, supposedly the result of willing buyers and willing sellers, included the activity of private carriers that were owned by grain companies. (By this time Cargill, Continental, ADM, Bunge and other grain giants all had their own barge fleets.) The bid and ask, the buyer and seller, ended up in some cases shaking hands with themselves. But that bid was purported to be the "fair market" rate for that day, like the world price of gold or West Texas crude. The grain traders had taken over the pricing of the river freight business just as barge building had surged.

CHAPTER 12

THE ADM TWO-STEP

Export grain traffic from the U.S. heartland grew through the 50s to the 80s (despite two brief presidential embargoes), because of an expanding world population and a concurrent growth in the global economy. From just the river ports in Minnesota, at the northern end of navigation, the tonnage of export grain by barge went from 124,000 tons in 1950 to over 10 million tons by 1980.

It was no wonder that barge lines involved with grain transport prospered and expanded. However, buying barge transportation from independent carriers on a negotiated and steadily increasing rate basis had the effect of driving bamboo shoots under the fingernails of grain traders. The grain guys didn't have that broad-based "board of trade" type of barometer for barge line rates. Nor did they with railroad rates. But the railroads owned their own right-of-way and couldn't be manipulated. There was no right of free entry on the rails as there was on the public waterways.

Cargill, always an innovator, had its own barge line and bought any excess transportation needs from independent barge lines. But with their own barge line they were not paying a river transportation profit to someone else. Their own barges and towboats were just a part of the cost of doing business, and with their own private barge line they cut out the carrier's middleman profit. As traffic grew, ADM, Continental, Bunge, Peavey, the farm co-ops and other major international grain traders got into the act of building their own fleets. Despite their efforts to contain transportation cost, it took some years for the private-carrier fleets to get near parity with the independent barge lines.

Archer-Daniels-Midland (ADM) began assembling its own fleet in the early 1970s. That subsidiary was called American River Transportation Co. (ARTCO), and ADM hired Neville Stone as CEO. Stone was a former World War II aviator, a gentleman Kentuckian who had previously been with Crounse Corporation and Upper Mississippi Towing Corp. During industry meetings and with his brief tenure in Minneapolis we had become close friends, hunting and fishing together. So it was not unusual that we did business together after he took over the helm of ARTCO.

In the mid 1970s Neville proposed that Twin City Shipyard build 200 covered hopper barges for ARTCO, 100 of which they would lease back to TCB for the exclusive carriage of ADM grain products. The remainder of our new, but growing, hopper barge fleet, numbering some 100-plus, would also be available for ADM cargo on a preferred basis. At this point in time, barge freight rates from the Upper Mississippi to Gulf ports were well above the old benchmark rate of 1975, about $6.00 per ton, and climbing. (It would eventually reach over 200% of that rate by 1981.) TCB agreed with Stone to establish a median freight rate for ARTCO in the 150% ($9.00 per ton) area: a rate that would not fluctuate up or down with barge supply and demand. It was, we considered, a win for both firms. There was no written contract. None was needed among friends.

However, with the influx of investor barges in the late 1970s and early 80s and the advent of barge freight trading on the St. Louis Merchants Exchange, the grain traders turned barges into a commodity and dictated ever-lowering freight rates that by 1982 were below barge-line costs, near $5.00 per ton. As disaster loomed for independent barge lines, my dear friend Neville Stone died after a short battle with cancer.

Mick Andreas, heir apparent to the ADM empire, first questioned our freight charges for grain to the Gulf, and I insisted on a meeting with his father, Dwayne Andreas, to confirm the TCB-ARTCO arrangement. Dwayne told me that he knew nothing of the deal I had crafted with Stone and said that ADM had to buy freight at "market," meaning, in effect, the artificial barge freight commodity market that the river grain traders had planted and fertilized. I pointed out that we had agreed to lease 100 barges from ADM on the assurance of sufficient freight revenue to service the lease. Now he was placing this revenue stream in jeopardy. He agreed to cancel the lease obligation and take back the barges. While this was some measure of relief, the overall situation in barge freight rates was suddenly a descending whirlpool for TCB's dry-bulk carrier operations, as it was with other independent barge lines.

Speaking before a 1982 convention of feed and grain dealers, I pointed out the dilemma that plunging barge income presented. Some traders shifted uneasily in their chairs, a few smirked, and one wonderful guy laughed loudly and shouted prophetically, "Yah, and you're going to eat below-cost rates for another 10 years." He was thrilled by the prospect of a massive bankruptcy of barge carriers. And as it turned out, he was an optimist.

Still other disasters were inexorably bearing down on the dry-cargo barge freight business. Southern Illinois-western Kentucky coal for public power generation was displaced by low-sulphur western coal, transported by unit trains. Then Midwest corn, formerly exported through the Gulf, began an unlikely metamorphosis into ethyl alcohol. The ethanol processing took place right in the farm belt, transported by a combination of rail, truck and barge, cutting deeply into export grain movement, largely the province of barge lines. Barged grain rates stayed generally at or below carrier's cost for the better part of 20 years.

The result of these successive tsunamis was the collapse of at least a dozen carriers, including TCB, and eventual consolidation of the swollen barge fleet into a few surviving barge lines. With an excess of some 4,000 hopper barges and attendant towboats, huge armadas were idled. Indeed, thousands of older barges, worth no more than scrap value, eventually found their way to South American rivers. In 1980, during the orgy of barge building, eight shipyards were devoted to hopper barge construction. Within three years only two remained.

Some of the major river carriers thought they could tough it out as the weaker ones perished, but they too suffered years of losses. The biggest, ACBL, had two reorganizations along the way. The failing contract grain carriers might well have prevailed against the grain traders' "restraint of trade," as defined in federal anti-trust law, but none had the resources for a protracted legal contest.

I had attempted to diversify by merging with both East-Coast and West-Coast carriers. But that could not cauterize the bleeding for TCB, and in 1983 I stepped aside. The coast partners crafted a dismantling of the conglomerate and the eventual bankruptcy of TCB river operations, harbor services, shipyard and terminal operations.

Chapter 13

River People

During my 30 years in the waterway business the members of the TCB family, notably Bob Maher, Dick Lambert, Bill Lambert, John Buursema, Ray Rauch, John McFarland and many others were dedicated, loyal, hardworking and blameless in its demise. Dick soldiered on to become an invaluable asset to the state of Minnesota as its director of Harbors and Waterways.

Those three decades on the river exposed me to dozens of unique characters: noble business people and distinguished river rats.

Joe Shiely Jr., a wonderful rascal, would phone me and invariably tell my secretary that he was Archbishop John Gregory Murray. The dear lady, my firewall against the rope salesmen, would inform me breathlessly that the archbishop was on the phone. It was ludicrous, because TCB had no connection with the Archdiocese of St. Paul, and in any event, John Gregory Murray had long since departed this vale of tears. It was like I was in a Monty Python skit.

I was privileged to know many other greats. Some already have entered this narrative, and many have departed for a land that knows no floods. I list them from memory in no particular order:

Wayne Musgrove: His Morgan City firm merged with TCB and went down with it, but he remained loyal and upbeat, a great entrepreneur and a prince among men.

Capt. Charlie Lehman: One of the few unpretentious riverboat captains, and author of "A Riverman's Lexicon," a language guide to the river.

Peter Fanchi: Former CEO of Federal Barge, one of the first to warn of the danger of investor barges.

Capt. Jack Moore: Port Captain of TCB operations in Chicago, a fine gregarious gentleman.

Fred Schulte: A charming and witty man who sold barges for Dravo and then Twin City Shipyard.

Dean Johnson: For many years friend and attorney to the Upper Mississippi barge fraternity.

Pat Yoder: A great lady and public affairs specialist, whose talents were largely wasted at the American Waterways Operators.

Steve Tell: Formerly with Upper Mississippi Towing Corp. and then with TCB, and a frequent hunting companion.

Jack Geary: CEO of Ohio River Co., a horseman and a great card player.

Joe Bobzien: A class guy who came to the helm of American Commercial Barge Line from the CSX empire.

Floyd Blaske: A sweet man from one of the founding families of river rats.

Frank Stegbauer: A gentleman and scholar from Southern Towing Co.

Berdon Lawrence: He kept both his oars in the liquid transportation business and was around until recently as chairman of Kirby.

Arnie Sobel: VP of water transport operations for Material Service Corp. of Chicago. A friend from the time TCB started in Chicago.

Bill Schmidt: Head of barge traffic for Bunge. Taught me how to "get-down-quick" in gin rummy.

John Donnelly: CEO of Ingram before the dry cargo business sank him and so many of us.

George Foster: Head of Jeff Barracks Marine, a great guy.

Marion Webb: Of Jeffboat and Louisville and a great hunting buddy.

Gerry Brown: Rose from the Cargill ranks to become CEO of Cargo Carriers, Inc. He enjoyed calling me a dinosaur, and now he's one.

Steve Golding: He bought our fleet of asphalt barges.

The Brent family of Greenville, Miss.: Pioneers in the business who stayed with liquid barging.

Tim Parker, Jr.: One of the surviving southern carriers that stuck with what they knew.

Bob Hougland: The "Duke of Paducah," whose dad and uncle were river men.

Carl Genz: Traffic manager with Great Northern Oil (later Koch) and a hunting chum.

Tom Gladders: A fine guy from a great river family.

Neal Diehl: Formerly of Ohio Barge Line and Ingram. Left us much too soon.

Nelson Spencer: He and the *Waterways Journal* family have kept us all informed and linked through the decades.

❖ ❖ ❖

Bless 'em all.

Then there were the SOBs. I shall not list them. You know who you are.

If you did not make the "greats" list or get mentioned in the text, just mark it down to my failing memory. I used to keep the location of 400 barges and several towboats in my head at one time. I was multi-tasking before the term was invented. Now I have trouble frying one egg and two Little Sizzlers while making the coffee.

Troubled Waters

Troubled Waters